Preface

The book MOULD DESIGN & PROCESSING HANDBOOK is prepared to help moulders to understand the role of material & mould. There are many publications to produce moulded articles including blow moulded articles, injection moulded articles and so on but this publication provides the information for the very first time about design and tooling aspects such as Properties of plastics, Mould steels for plastic mouldes, Injection mould design, Compression & transfer mould design, Blow mould design, Standard mould bases & Parts, Conversion tables etc. Properties of plastics chapter includes Injection moulding temperature, Injection moulding pressure, mould linear shrinkage, specific gravity. Injection design chapter includes determination of number of cavities based on the machine capacity, selection of the injection moulding machine, strength of cavity, thermal properties of plastics, recommended fits used in injection and compression mould, mould cooling, ejection system. The other chapters also cover the most important informations for moulders. Keeping in view all these aspects, this book has been written comprising relevant information on the subject. This is equally good for carrying out mould design & data.

I thank to all those who have extended their valuable co-operation in the completion of this book.

Director

ENGINEERS INDIA RESEARCH INSTITUTE

Nai Sarak, New Delhi.
E-Mail : eirisidi@bol.net.in

CONTENTS AND SUBJECT INDEX

MOULDS DESIGN & PROCESSING HAND BOOK

The Book covers complete details of Mould Design & Processing with Diagrams etc to understand the technology of moulds.

Compiled by :

EIRI CONSULTANTS & ENGINEERS

Identification & Evaluation Division for *HI-TECH PROJCETs* from last 23 years

ENGINEERS INDIA RESEARCH INSTITUTE

4449, Nai Sarak, Main Road, Delhi - 110 006 (INDIA)

•Ph.: 3918117,3916431,3920361,3960797 •Fax: 91-11-3916431

•E-mail : eirisidi@bol.net.in •Website : www.eikotech.com/eiri.htm

ALSO AT :

4/27, Roop Nagar, Near Roop Nagar No.1 School, New Delhi - 7

• Ph : 392 0361, 396 0797, 391 8117, 391 6431

PRINTED & PUBLISHED BY

ENGINEERS INDIA RESEARCH INSTITUTE

4449, Nai Sarak, Main Road, Delhi - 110 006 (INDIA)

●Ph. : 3918117, 3916431, 3920361, 3960797 ● Fax : 91-11- 391 6431, 396 0797

●E-mail : eirisidi@bol.net.in ●Website : www.eikotech.com/eiri.htm

DISTRIBUTED BY

INDIAN INSTITUTE OF CONSULTANTS, ROOP NAGAR, DELHI - 7

ISBN :81 - 86732 - 23 - 3

Printed in New Delhi (INDIA)

Rs. 495

Printed & Published by **Sudhir Gupta** for **"Engineers India Research Institute"** and Laser Type Set by **VIJAY GUPTA**, at **Engineers India Research Institute,** Nai Sarak and printed at **Affif printers,** Lal Kuan, Delhi - 6

1

MOULDS

What is Mould?

The **MOULD** is a robust construction consisting of two parts, one male (core) and the other female (cavity). The space between core and cavity (when the mould is closed and clamped) is filled with plastic melt during injection stroke.

The **MOULD** for parts with undercut, hole / slot, require sliding core / collapsible side cheeks mechanism. The stiff threaded parts require unscrewing mechanism in the mould.

Parts may incorporate metal or plastic inserts, holes and internal and external threads.

The moulds also incorporate cooling system and ejection mechanism. The mould is normally cooled by circulating cold / chilled water or even oil.

The cost of mould increase with increased complication in shape and precision.

You must refer chapter on Mould for greater details.

What are the function of Injection mold and how these function are carried out?

Function of the injection mould is

- accommodation and distribution of melt.
- shaping, cooling and solidification of the melt..
- ejection of the moulded parts.

Other mechanical functions are

- accommodation of forces.
- transmission of motion
- alignment of mould components.

The above mentioned function can be carried out with the help of following functional system.

- Sprue, runner and gate system for conveying the melt to cavity,
- Cavity to provide outer surface of moulded part,
- Heat exchange system to extract excess heat to maintain heat balance and desired mould temperature,
- Ejection system for ejection (removal) of moulded parts from the mould.
- Guiding and locating system for alignment of mould components.

- Machine platen mounting arrangements,
- Mould plates and components designed to withstand the forces in the mould cavity.
- Transmission of motions during mould close / open stroke to relieve the moulded parts to facilitate easy ejection.

Ejection system can be decided on the basis of part geometry and it is housed in the moving half of the mould.

- without undercuts
- with internal undercuts'
- with external undercuts

Ejection of moulded part could be

- pushed out with the help of ejector pins mounted on an ejector plate.
- stripped with rotation of threaded core either by rack and pinion mechanism or small motor driven mechanism.

Why mould is considered as Tool? What is the size of the mould? What are the types of Mould?

A mould provides the desired shape and dimensions to the polymer. Therefore it is a tool.

The size of the mould depends on

- shape and dimensions of part
- number of cavities
- quantity of production desired.

The mould consists of

- Injection half (fixed half) sub assembly
- moving half sub assembly.

In the shut condition i.e. Mould closed, an empty space is formed between core and cavity surface of the Mould. This space includes parts as well as sprue and runner system. This space is filled by plastic melt in the injection moulding machine process.

The parts with undercut or hollow space will demand special provision in the mould to move the under cut portion of the part on taper pin during mould open operation, similarly hollow parts will require core pull arrangement on the mould. These features of the parts will require larger sized mould.

There are various types of moulds

- **Two plate mould**

The two-plate mould is the simplest simple cavity mould where in cores half and cavity half open to eject the moulded part. The sprue it self acts as gate in such moulds.

- **Three plate mould**

Three-plate mould is used for multicavity moulds. In this type of mould two partition or separation take place during mould open operation. The first separation where runners are located so that sprue is separated from moulded part. The second separation, which takes place after the first separation has already occurred, ejects the moulded parts.

What is Hot Runner Mould?

Hot runner, insulated runner etc. are actually extension of machine nozzle inside the mould. This system does not produce moulded runner. Hence it avoids wastage in runners. A typical mould is shown in fig.

What is the classification of mould?

- **Stripper plate moulds** where moulded parts are ejected by stripper plate.
- **Slide mould** with sliding components moved on inclined cam pin to facilitate release of moulded part from the cavity.
- **Split cavity mould** where cavity opens up to release the moulded part as the mould opens. Suitable for external threaded parts.
- **Mould with unscrew arrangement.** The thread-forming core is rotated by built - in mecanism actuated by mould open stroke.

What are the elements of mould?

Sprue bush: It provides passage for melt from machine nozzle' to the parting surface. It consists of a tapered bore. The smaller bore diameter should be slightly more than the bore diameter of nozzle. At the contact point of nozzle with sprue bush a sperical radius is provided which is slightly more than the bore diameter of nozzle.

Locating ring : It is fitted as the fixed half of the mould. Projected portion of the locating ring fits into a counterbore on fixed platen of the machine. It also aligns the sprue bush of the mould with the center of the mould as well as machine platen.

Runner : It is a channel machined in one or both mould plates to deliver the melt from sprue to cavity through gate.

Gate : It is the opening, which connects the runner to the cavity. There are various types of gates.

Fixed half : The half of the mould fixed to the platen of the machine is known as Fixed half. It is also knows as injection half of the mould.

Moving half : It is the order half of the mould, which is fitted to the moving platen of the machine.

Cavity : It is that part of mould, which gives the outside dimensions of the moulded part. It can be an insert, fitted on cavity plate.

INJECTION MOULD

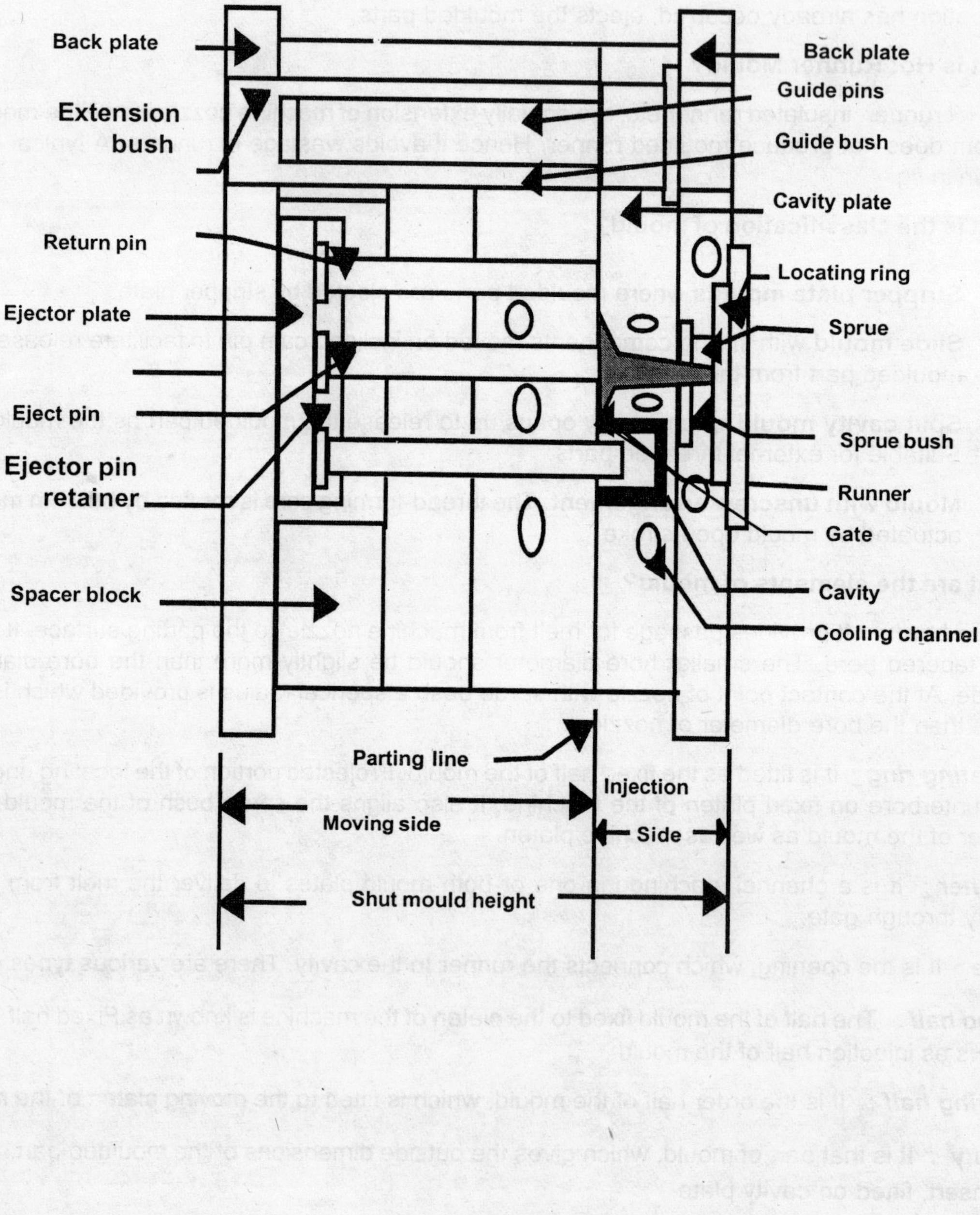

NON SELF DEGATING TWO PLATE MOULD

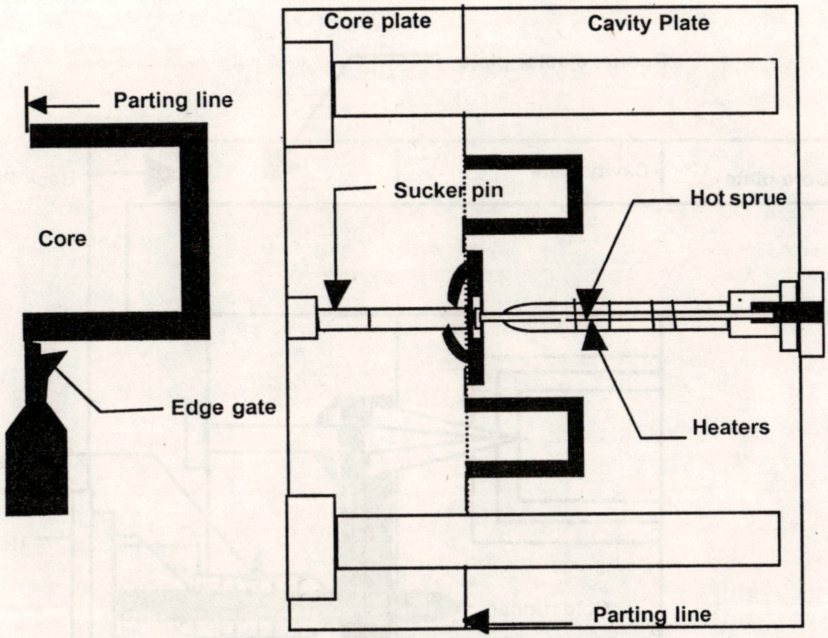

SELF DEGATING TWO PLATE MOULD

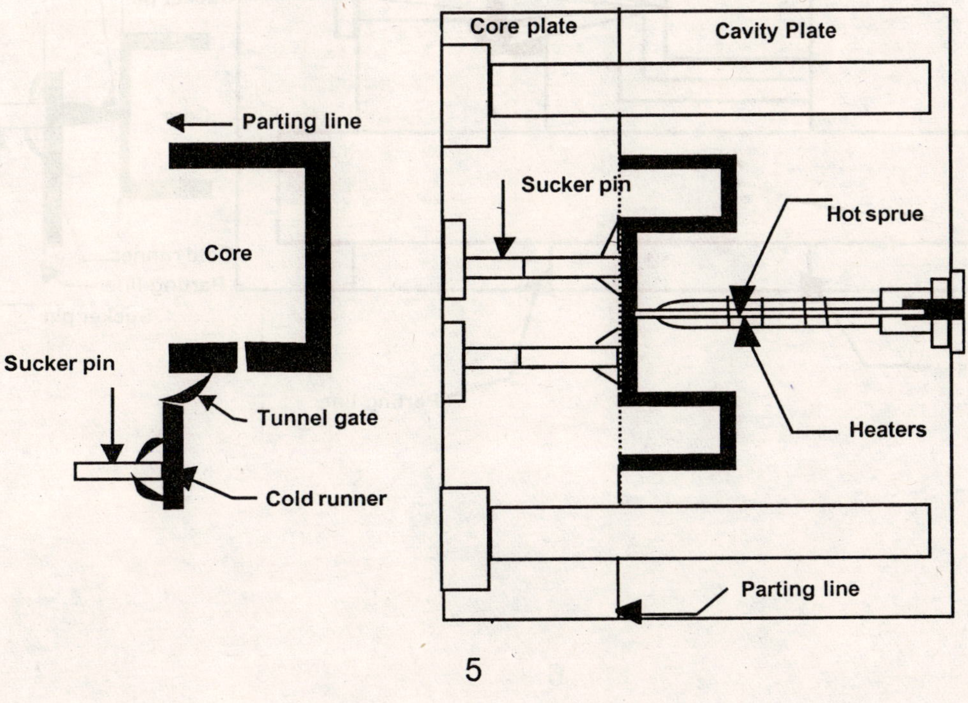

THREE PLATE INJECTION

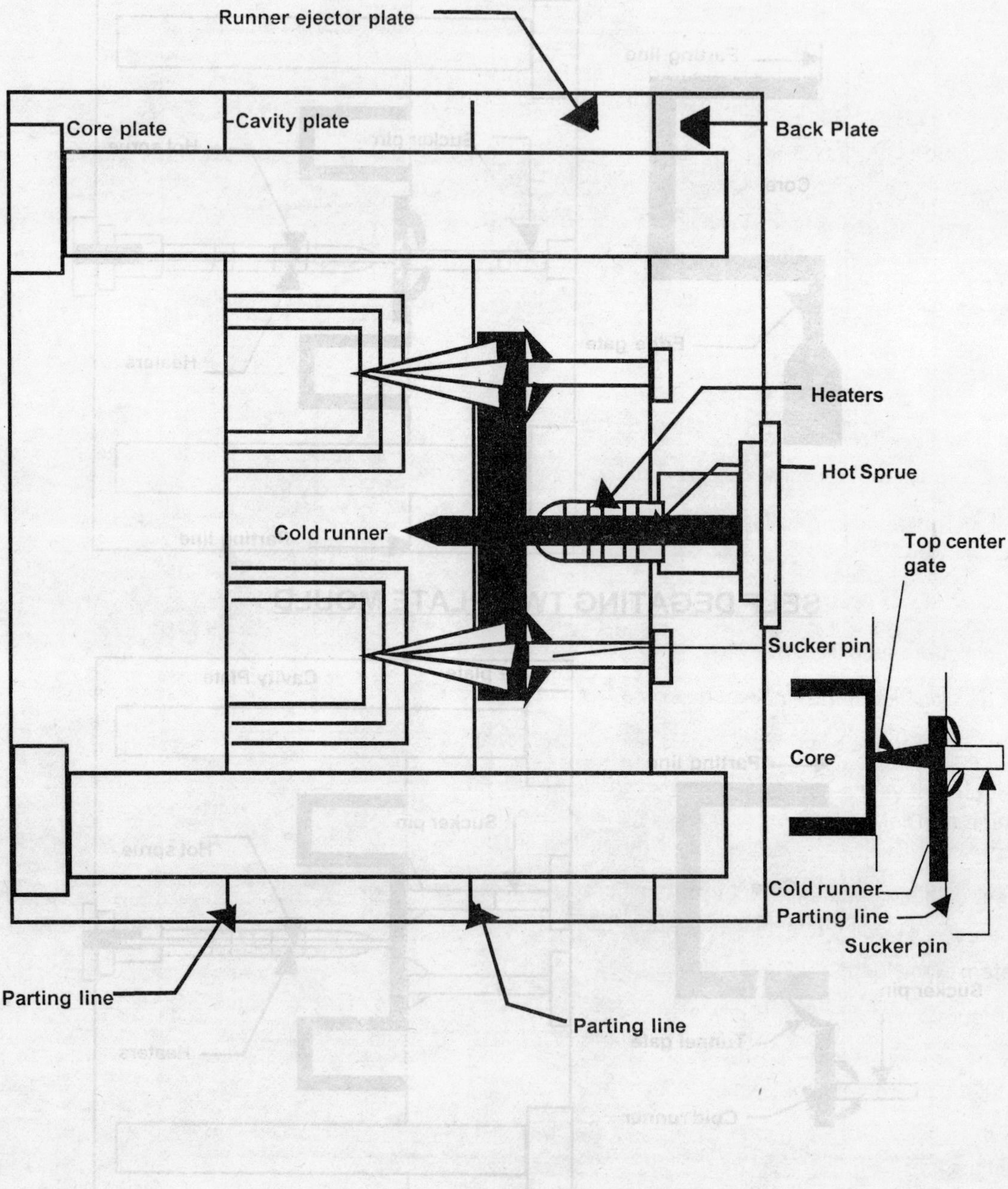

INSULATED RUNNER MOULD

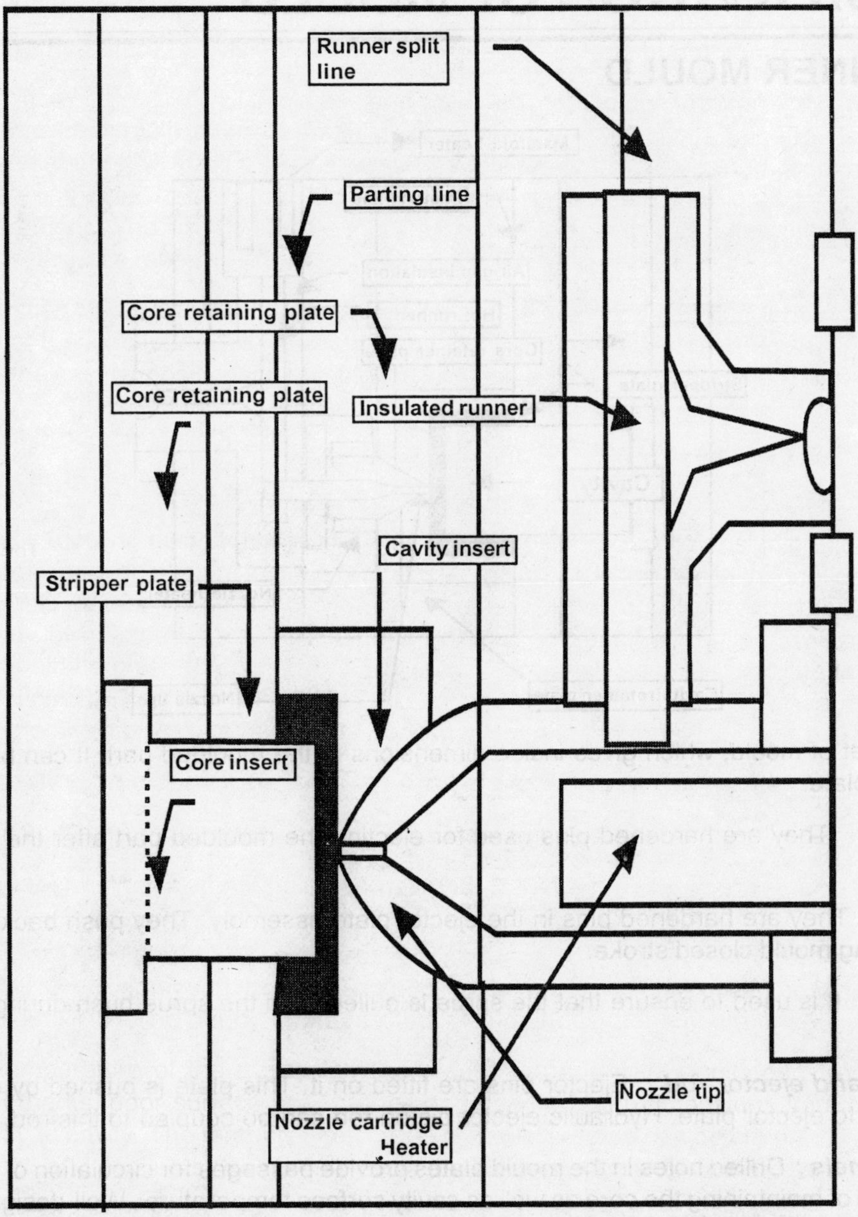

2

CLASSIFICATION OF MOULD

HOT RUNNER MOULD

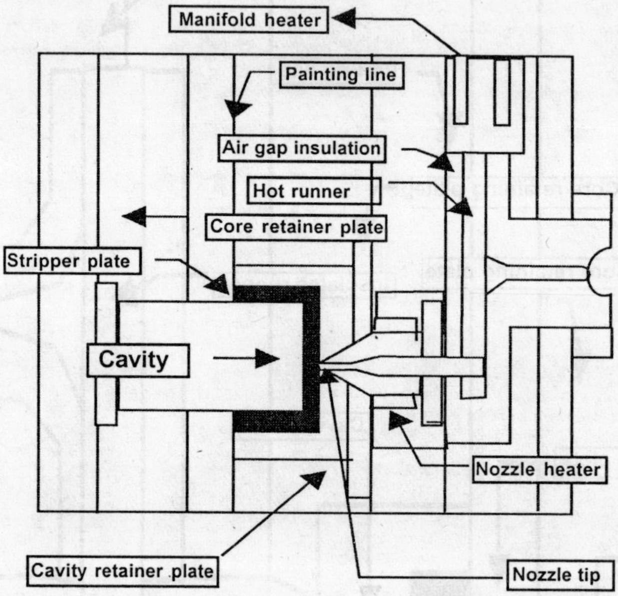

Core : It is that of mould, which gives inside dimensions of the moulded part. It can be an insert, fitted on core plate.

Ejector Pins : They are hardened pins used for ejecting the moulded part after the moulded is opened.

Return pins : They are hardened pins in the ejector plate assembly. They push back the ejector assembly during mould closed stroke.

Sprue puller : It is used to ensure that the sprue is pulled from the sprue bush during the mould open stroke.

Ejector plate and ejector rod : Ejector pins are fitted on it. This plate is pushed by ejector rod, which is fitted, to ejector plate. Hydraulic ejector piston rod can be coupled to this rod.

Cooling channels : Drilled holes in the mould plates provide passages for circulation of oil or water for the purpose of maintaining the core as well as cavity surface temperature . Well-designed cooling channels can reduce the cycle time.

Guide pins (Leader pins) and guide bushes : The maintain the wall thickness between core and cavity it is necessary to align these. This is achieved by providing guide pillars in one half of the mould and guide bushes in the other half of the mould. Guide pillars also supports the weight of floating plates.

Locating pulgs : Locating plugs provide location and alignment of the core and cavity for obtaining accurate dimensions.

Back Plate : It is the plate fitted behind the core plate. It prevent core plate from bending under high injection pressure in cavity.

Spacers : Spacers are mounted between back plate and support plate. It provides space for ejector assembly.

What is the feed system in the mould? What are the factors to be considered for feed system?

The passage to convey the plastic melt from nozzle of machine to cavity is knows as feed system. It includes sprue, main runner, branch runner and gate.

While designing feed system following considerations should not be ignored,

- ***Shape of runner .*** It should offer least resistance to flow and minimum heat loss. Trapezoidal shape is most popular.
- ***Size of runner*** depends on
- Volume of moulding and wall thickness.
- Runner size increases in direct proportion to the volume of moulding.
- Viscosity of melt. Higher viscosity demands higher sized runner.
- Longer the runner length, the more is the heat and pressure loss. To make up for this runner size has to be increased.
- Runner size should be between 2mm and 10mm diameter only.
- For moulded parts of tight tolerances the feed system should be balanced, It means that the melt should reach all the cavities at the same time and it will have identical cavity pressure profile in all the cavities so that each moulded part from all the cavities are absolutely same in all respect. This will result in same shrinkage and same weight in all the cavities.
- Balanced runner suystem can be achieved by
- Equal length of runner to all cavities.
- Runner of increasing cross-section to compensate the loss in pressure.
- Runner of uniform size but the gate of different sizes.
- The gate closer to sprue should be smallest and furrthest from sprue should be largest.
- The gate is the opening of runner into the cavity.

What is Got? What are the types of gate?

Plastic melt enters the cavity through the Gate. There are various types of gate.

STRIPPER PLATE EJECTION

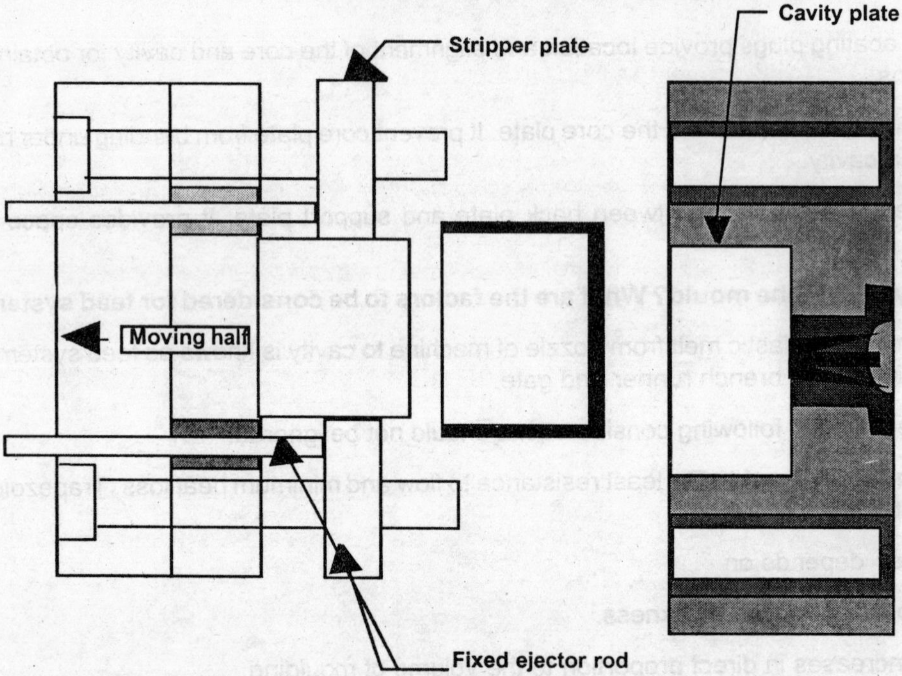

General purpose gates.

Sprue gate for simple cavity-suitable for large and central feeding. Degating is difficult card a mark is left after degating.

Rectangular gate : It is general -purpose gate.

Gates for tubular parts

Ring gaste : The melt enters around the core. It facilitates easy melt flow and avoids wels lines. Degating is difficult.

Disc or diaphragm gate : The melt enters the cavity through thin passage all around the inner diameter from the runner in the shape of disc.

Gates for avoiding jetting effect

over - lap gate : The gate is positioned in such a way (as shown in the diagram) so that of the jetting effect is avoided. Degating is difficult and leaves a mark.

Tab gate : An additional tab or projection is provided on the part. The runner meets the tab through a rectangular gate at 90 angle. The sharp 90 degree turn prevents jetting effect.

Gates for thin walled parts

Fan gate:- It is recommended for box like pats. The gate passage is thin (narrow) and wide so that the melt spreads from the gate to wider region in the cavity thus reducing the possibility of flow times.

Film gate: The gate passage is very thin and its width covers the entire edge of the part. The chances of warpage in thin walled part in reduced with this type of gate.

Self cutting gates

Pin gate: It is recommended for control feeding multicavity moulds. It requires 3- plate mould design. The gate in circular tapering towards the part.

Submarine gate or Tunnel gate: It opens into the cavity below the parting surface. Degating takes place mould open strokes or ejection.

What is the classification of Moulds?

CLASIFICATION OF MOULDS

CHARACTERISTICS DEPENDENT UP ON DESIGN	CHARACTERISTICS DEPENDENT UP ON MOULDING
- Transmission of motion - Ejection system - Number of parting lines - Alignment - Transmission of force - Moulding to machine platen	- Cavity - Cavity lay-out - Sprue & runner system - Slides and lifters - Ejection system

DISTINCTION OF MOULDS ACCORDING TO PRIMARY DESIGN FEATURES

DISTINCTION ACCORDING TO	INFLUENCING FACTORS	DESIGN VERSION	MOULD DESIGNATION
Number of parting lines	• Geometry of moulding • Number of cavities • Type of gates • Ejection principle	• 2 Plate mould • 3 plate mould • stripper plate mould	• Standard mould • Degating mould • stripper mould • Stack mould
Ejection system	• Shape of moulding • Polymer used • Processing parameters • Lot size	• Slides • Split cavity • Unscrewing type • Stripper plate	• Slide mould • Split cavity mould • Unscrewing mould • Stripper mould
Heat exchange system	• Injection moulding machine • Cycle time • Plastic material • Economics	• Hot manifold • Insulating runner	• Hot runner • mould • Insulated runner mould
Transmission of forces	• • Rigidity of mould • Geometry of moulding • Injection pressure • Plastic material	• Split cavity • Interlock • Leader pins	• Split cavity mould • Standard mould

CRITERIA LEADING TO A CHARACTERISTIC MOULD DESIGNATION

DESIGNATION	CRITERIA
1- Standard mould	Simplest design, one parting line, derectional opening motion, demoulding primarily by gravity, with ejector pins or sleeve.
2- Stripper mould	Similar to (1) but demoulding with stripper plate.
3- Slide mould	One parting line, opening motion in main direction and transverse with slide actuated by cam pin.
4- Auto separation of runner & moulding	Similar to (1) but separation of runner & moulding by cutting with additional plate moving transverse (like3).
5- Split cavity mould	One parting line, opening motion in main direction and transverse, cavity halves slide on inclined planes can withstand lateral forces.
6- Unscrewing mould	Rotational motion for automatic unscrewing of moulding is mechanically actuated.
7- Two stage opening mould	Two parting lines for demoulding runner & mouldings separately, One directional opening motion in two stages.
8- Stack mould	Cavity plate stacked with several parting lines.
9- Insulated runner mouls	Two parting lines, no conventional runner system but channels with enlarged cross section permitting formation of a hot core insulated by a surrounding frozen skin.
10- Hot runner mould	Runner is lacated in electrically heated manifold.
11- Special mould	Combination (2) to (10) for moulding with special requirements which do not permit simple solution.

What is the role of feed system - Sprue & Runner ?

It has to deliver the melt through the gate into the mould. Smaller cross section will result in increased loss of pressure and larger cross section will result in increase of scrap and also increase in cooling time.

Highly viscose polymer will require larger (cross section) sized sprue and runner. Runner system should be designed for balanced flow. It will give better dimesional tolerance.

Runner system depends on the cavity layout. Injection axis is normally at the center of fixed platen of machine. Therefore cavities have to be arranged around central sprure so that following conditions be fulfilled.:

- All cavities should be filled at the same time with melt of same temperature and viscosity.
- The flow length of runner should be short to maintain minimum scrap.
- The distance between cavities should be sufficient to accommodate cooling lines and ejector pins. There must adequate cross section to withstand the injection force.

TYPES OF RUNNER LAYOUT

LAY OUT TYPE	ADVANTAGE	DISADVANTAGE
CIRCULAR	Equal flow lengths to all cavities, Easy ejection,	Only limited number of cavities can be accommodated.
SERIES	Space for more cavities than circular layout.	Unequal flow lengths to individual cavities, uniform filling can be possible with corrected runner/gate dimensions.
SYMMETRICAL	Equal flow lengths to all cavities with out gate correction.	Large runner volume, more scrap, rapid cooling of melt, Hot runner system is recommended to overcome the large volume of scrap.

FACTORS AFFECTING RUNNER SYSTEM

MOULDING	MATERIAL
Geometry Volume wall thickness	Viscosity Amorphous or crystalline filler Freezing time..
Quality requirements Dimensional, Optical, Mechanical,	Softening range, Softening temperature, Sensitivity to heat, Shrinkage,
MOULDING MACHINE	**INJECTION MOULD**
Type of clamping, Injection pressure, Ijection rate.	Automatic ejection, Manual ejection, Temperature of runner system.

DEMANDS OF RUNNER SYSTEM

1.	Cavity filling with minimum	6.	Length as short as possible to keep losses in pressure, temperature and material small.
2.	Restrictions to flow as few as possible.	7.	Cross section so large that freezing time equals or slightly exceeds that of moulding. Only then can holding pressure can remain effective until part is solid.
3.	share of total shot weight as small as possible	8.	Runner system should have little or no effect on cycle time.
4.	Ease of ejection.	9.	Place gating at the thickest section of part.
5.	Appearance of part should remain unaffected.	10.	Location or design of gate such as to prevent jetting.
		11.	Location or design of gate such as to give straight & uniform streams in all direction so that is filled in balanced manner.

FACTORS AFFECTING RUNNER

1	Part volume	6	Surface volume ratio	11	Cost of manufacturing
2	Wall thickness	7	Heat losses	12	Type of muld Hot/cold runner
3	Polymer	8	Frictional losses		
4	Length of flow	9	Cooling time		
5	Resistance to flow	10	Amount of scrap		

FUNCTIONS OF RUNNER

1	Conveying melt rapidly and unrestricted in to cavity in shortest way and with minimum of heat and pressure loss.
2	Melt must enter cavity (cavities) the gates at the same time under the same pressure and with same temperature.
3	For resons of material saving, cross sections should be kept small. Larger cross section can increase cooling time.
4	The surface-over volume ratio should be kept as small as possible.

CROSS SECTIONS OF RUNNERS

CIRCULAR CROSS SECTION

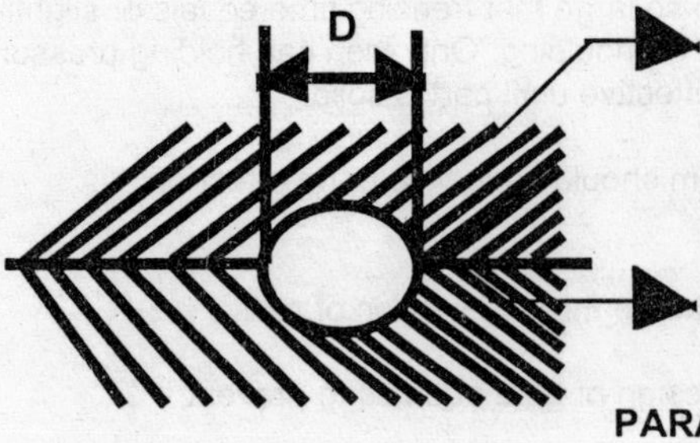

Advantages :
Smallest surface relative to cross section, slowest cooling rate low heat & frictional losses, center of channel freezes last - therefore effective holding pressure.

Disadvantages :
Machining into both halves of the mould is difficult and expensive.

PARABOLIC CROSS SECTION

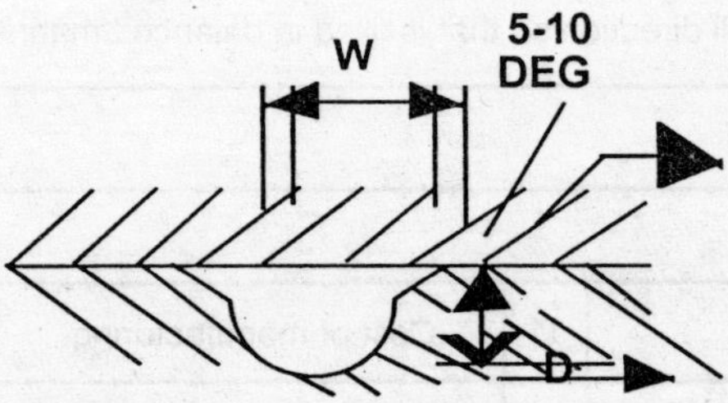

Advantage
Best approximate of circular cross section, simpler machining in one half of mould- movable side- for reasons of ejection.

Disadvantages :
More heat losses & scrap compared to

TRAPEZOIDAL CROSS SECTION

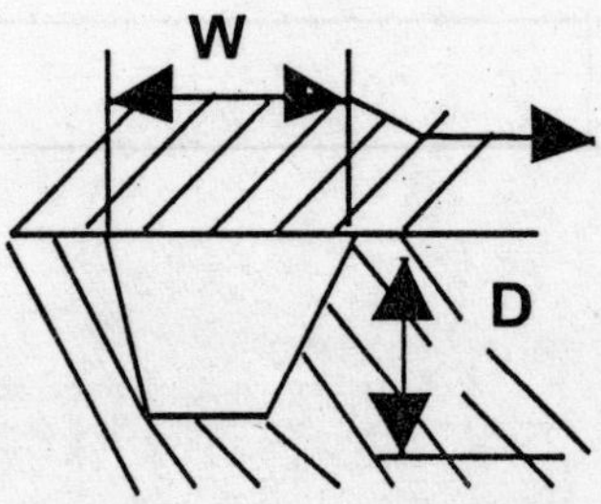

Alternative to parabolic cross - section.
Disadvantages:
More heat losses & scrap compared to parabolic crosssection.

RECTANGLE & SEMI CIRCLE CROSS SECTION - UNFAVORABLE

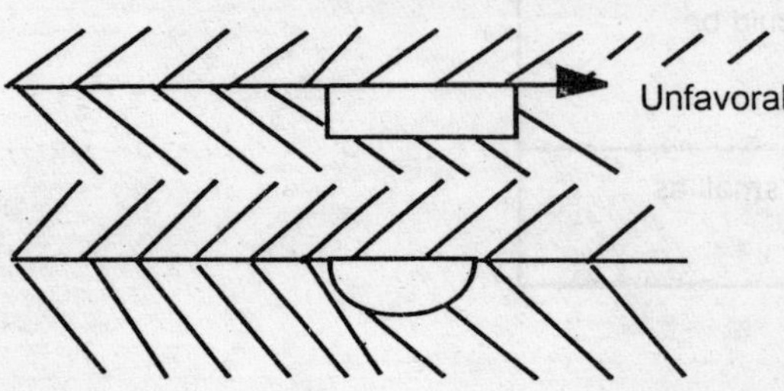

Unfavorable cross sections must be avoided.

RUNNER SYSTEM

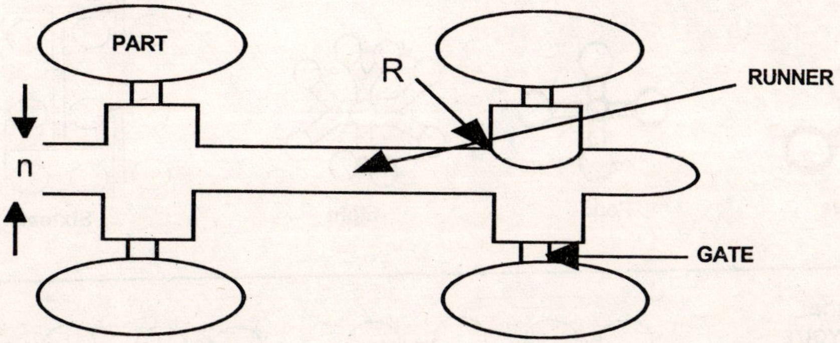

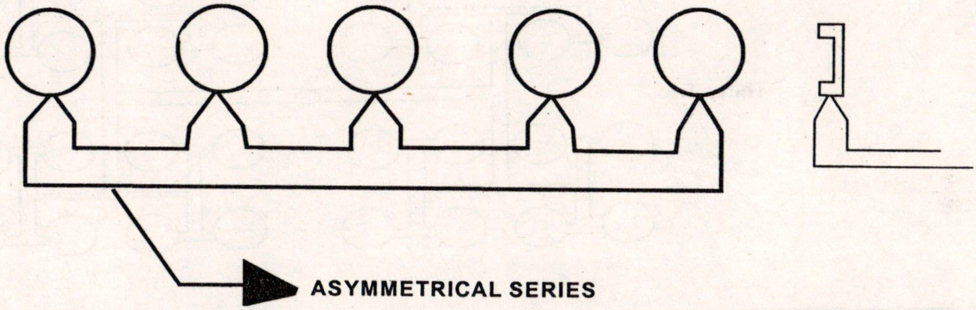

ASYMMETRICAL SERIES

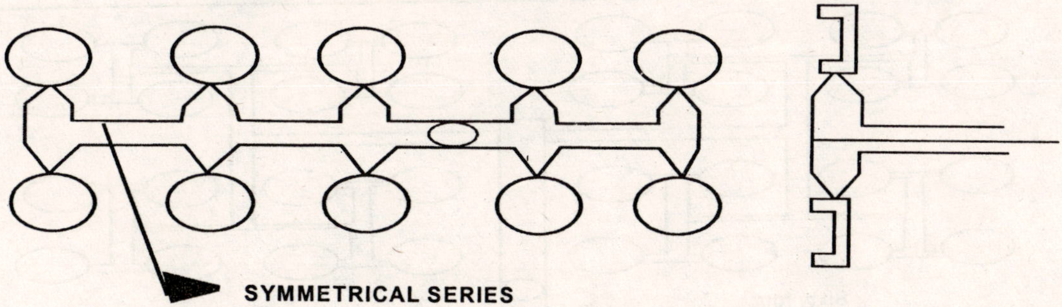

SYMMETRICAL SERIES

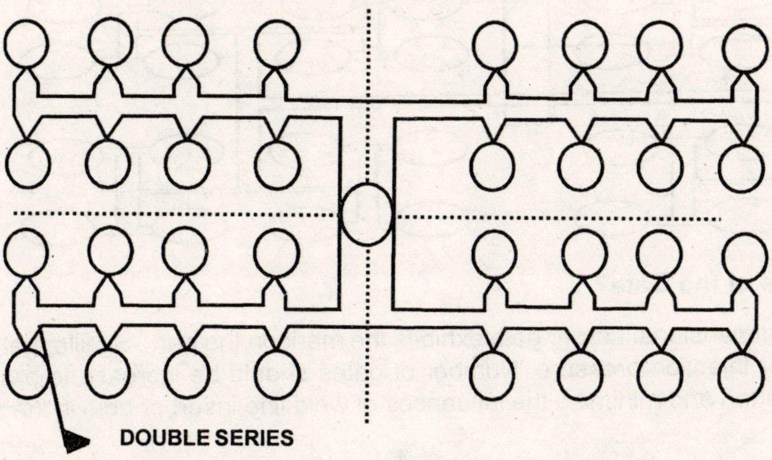

DOUBLE SERIES

BALANCED RUNNER SYSTEM

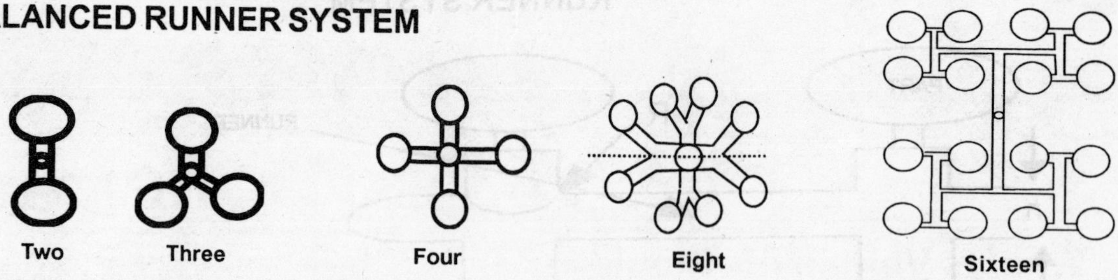

SYMMETRICAL
CAVITY LAYOUT

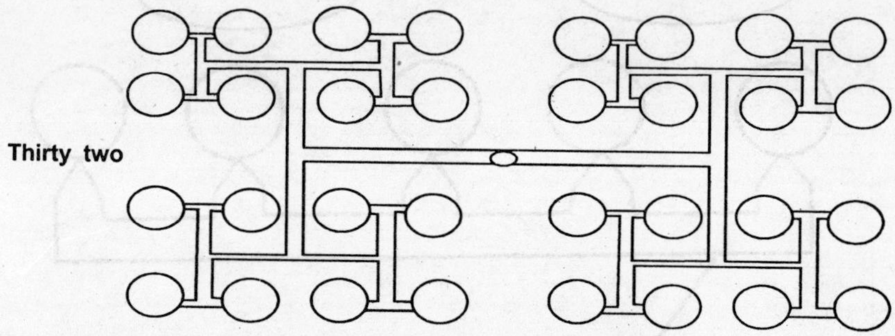

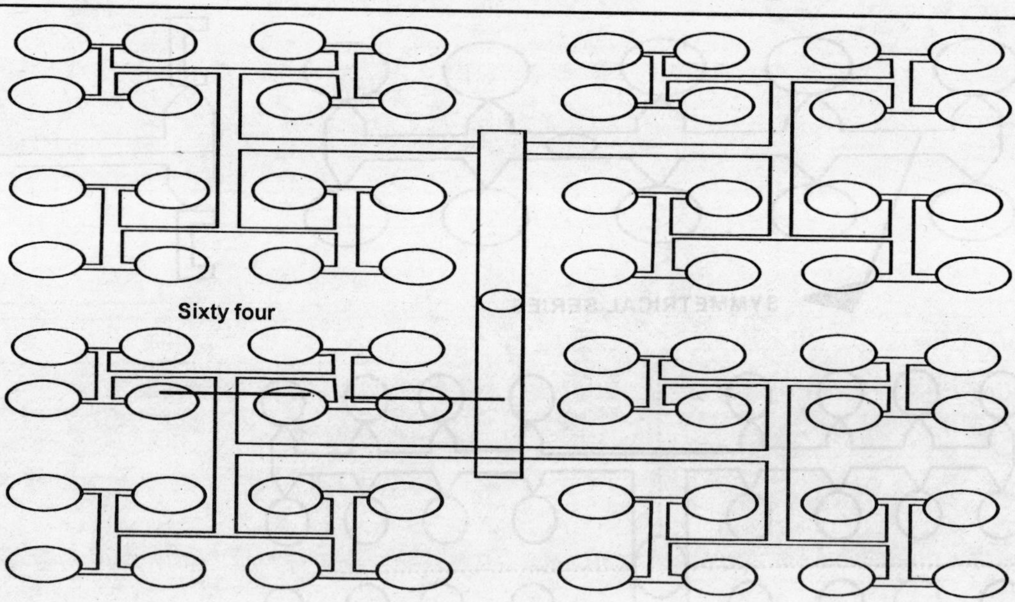

What are the limitations of the Gate?

It should have adequate dimensions. Larger gate exhibits the mark on the part . Similler gate on the mould will demand higher injection pressure. Number of gates should be increase to provide uniform and balanced flow patten and minimise the influences of weld line insert or hole in the part.

3

VENT IN THE MOULD

What is Vent in the mould?

While injecting the melt, the air from the mould is required to be expelled. The rate of air escape should be equal to the rate of injection. If the rate of injection increase then the air is trapped in the cavity and it causes melt to burn with black marks. It also requires higher injection pressure to overcome the resistance due to air trap. The proper air vent in the mould will enable it to fill easily at lower pressure without any defect

FACTORS AFFECTING GATES	
MOULDED PARTS	● GEOMETRY ● WALL THICKNESS ● DIRECTION OF MECHANICAL LOADING ● QUALITY DEMANDS WITH RESPECT TO DIMENSIONS, COSMETICS, MECHANICS. ● FLOW LENGTH/WALL THICKNESS RATIO
POLYMERS	● VISCOSITY ● TEMPERATURE ● FLOW CHARACTERISTICS ● FILLERS ● SHRINKAGE
GENERALITIES	● DISTORTION ● WELD LINE ● EASE OF EJECTION ● SEPARAION FROM MOULDING ● COSTS

GATES - CLASSIFICATION

RUNNERS WHICH REMAIN WITH MOULDING & IT REQUIRES TO BE CUT OFF:

- SPRUE GATE
- PINPOINT GATE
- EDGE GATE
- DISK GATE
- RING GATE

RUNNERS WHICH ARE AUTOMATICALLY REMOVED FROM THE MOULDING AND ARE EJECTED SEPARATELY.

- SUBMARINE GATE
- PINPOINT GATE WITH 3- PLATE MOULD

RUNNERS WHICH ARE AUTOMATICALLY SEPARATED FROM THE MOULDING BUT REMAIN WITH THE MOULD.

- PINPOINT GATE WITH REVERSED SPRUE,
- HOT RUNNER.
- INSULATED RUNNER.

DIFFERENT TYPES OF GATES

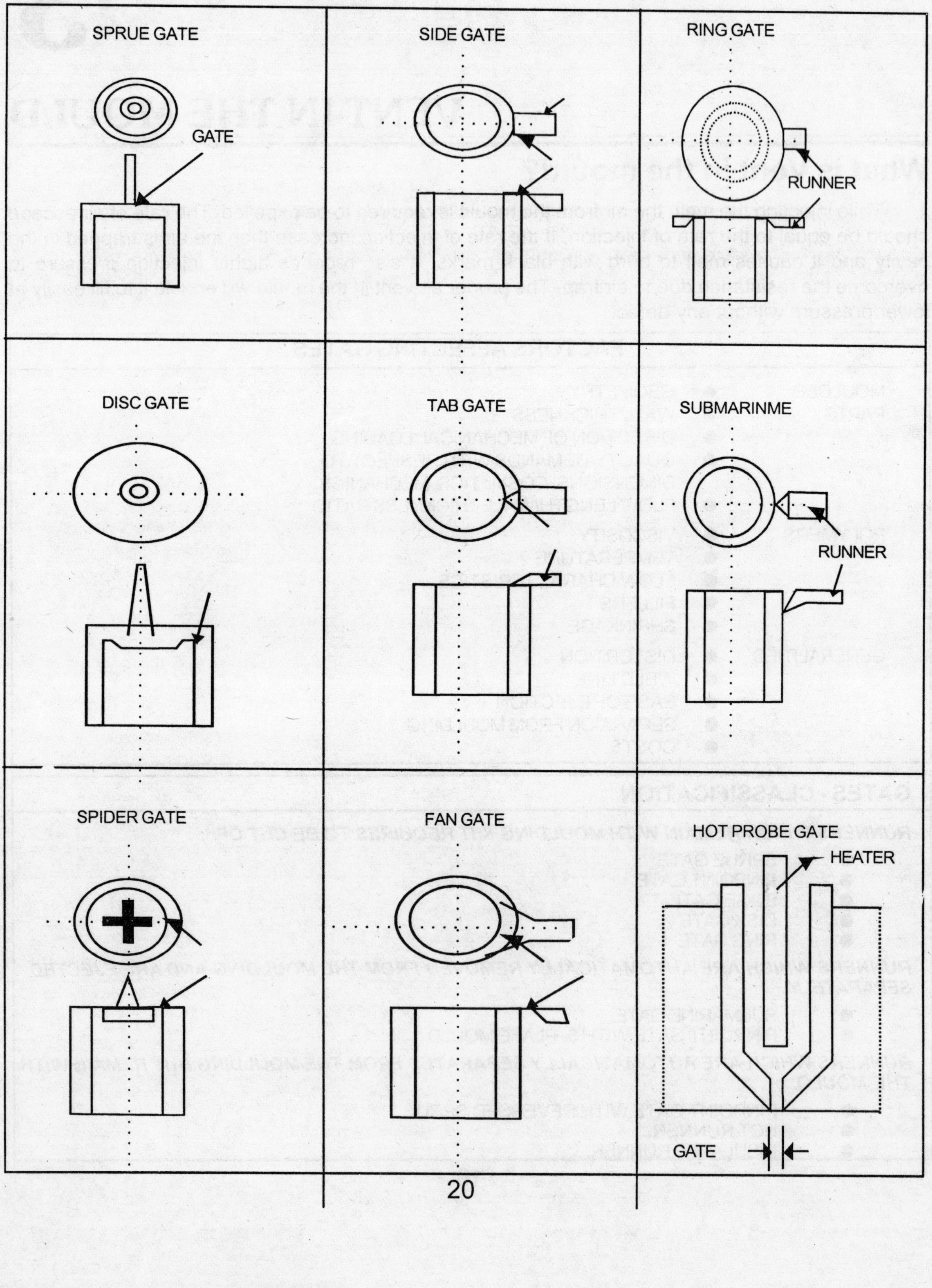

APPLICATION OF VARIOUS TYPES OF GATE

TYPE OF GATE	Application	Advantages	Disadvantages
SPRUE GATE	For temperature sensitive high viscouse materials, high quality parts and those with heavy sections.	High quality & exact dimensions	Post operation for sprue removel & visible gate mark.
EDGE GATE	For parts with large areas such as plate & strips	No weld lines, high quality, exact, dimensions.	Post operation of gate removal.
DISK GATE	For axially symmetrical parts with core supported at other end.	No weld lines, no reduction of strength.	Post operation of gate removal.
RING GATE	For sleeve like parts with parts with core supported ends.	Uniform wall no reduction of circumference.	Slight weld line, gate removal removal.
SUBMARINE GATE	For smaller parts in multicavity moulds & for elastic materials.	Automatic gate removal.	High pressure loss, for simple parts only.
PINPOINT GATE	For multicavity moulds & center gating	Automatic gate revomal.	Large volume of scrap - with 3 plate mould, higher mould cost.
HOT RUNNER	For high quality technical parts, independent of cycle time, suitable for materials difficult to process.	No material loss from runner system Automatic gate separation.	Expensive mould because of control equipment.

CROSS - SECTION OF GATES AND THEIR POSITION RELATIVE TO RUNNER

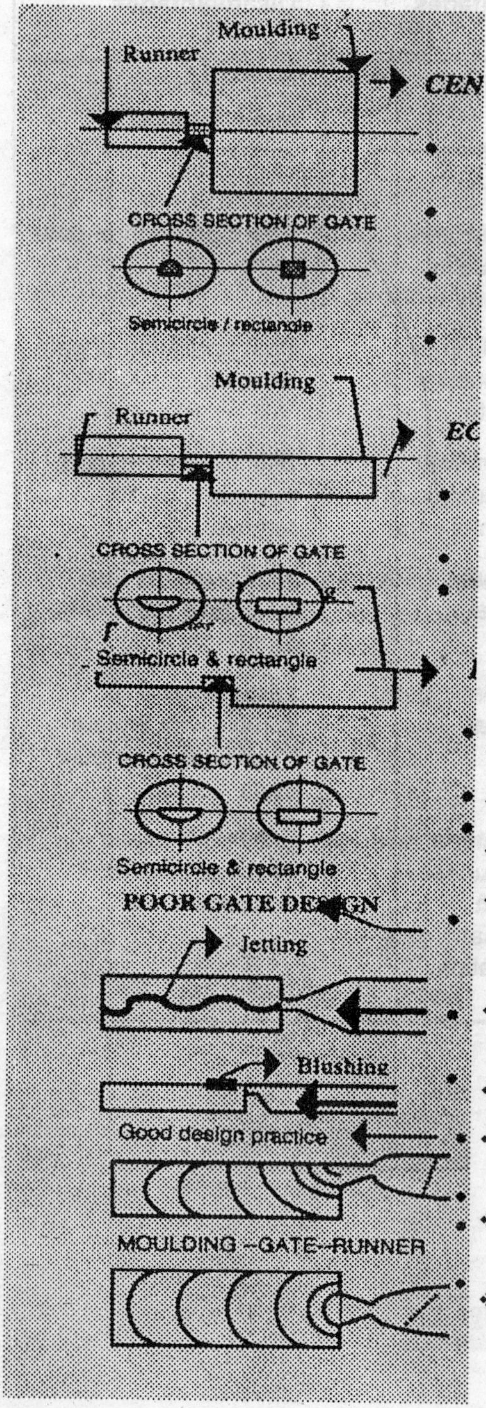

CENTRIC GATE

- ❖ Small surface to volume ratio of circular cross section reduces heat loss & friction.
- ❖ Difficult machining operation in both moulds halves needed. Cost for rectangle cross section is very high.
- ❖ Centric position position renders separation more difficult & requires post-moulding operation.
- ❖ Gate promotes jetting.

ECCENTRIC GATE

- ❖ The eccentric position of gate facilitates machining.
- ❖ Ease of ejection & separation from moulding.
- ❖ Gate position aligned to wall impedes jetting.

ECCENTRIC GATE

- ❖ The eccentric position of gate facilitates machining.
- ❖ Ease of ejection & separation from moulding.
- ❖ Gate position aligned to wall impedes jetting.
- ❖ Gate should be positioned in such a way that no jetting can occur causing troublesome marks. Melt must impinge on the wall or other obstacle.
- ❖ If gate is machined only into one half, cold skin may be carried into cavity resulting blush marks.
- ❖ Remedy : a special cold slug well accepts cold material.
- ❖ Centric location of gate with abrupt transition & rough walls prevent transport of cold surface layer.
- ❖ Radius at transition causes laminar flow of melts into caivity & prevents jetting.
- ❖ Radius at transition make gate removal more difficult. They should nevertheless, be preferred because of better flow conditions, which result in higher quality with respect to dimensions & mechanical strength.

What is the significance of wall thickness of part?

Injection moulding is normally ideal for parts with uniform wall thickness upto 4mm (maximum 6 mm). The cooling time is proportional to square of wall thickness. Therefore thicker walled part will have longer cooling time. Thinner wall thickness would require higher pressure to fill. When wall thickness is more, then gas injection moulding is recommended.

Designer of part should be in a position of adjusting or modifying wall thickness in order to achieve even spreading of melt flow stream. If flow path and wall thickness is not in a balanced ratio to one another, then there is a risk of warpage - at least in certain part of the moulding.

Very long flow paths, thin wall thickness and slow rate of filling due to incorrectly designed gates, cause premature recrystallisation of partially crystalline thermoplastics. This results in excessive shear and stretching of crystalline zones, which have already been reformed. Hence the moulded part will not have expected fracture resistance. Their dimensional stability at higher service temperature will be much reduced. The flow rate of the melt as it enters the cavity has a decisive influence on the flow path wall thickness ratio.

At the junction of different wall thickness, sink marks are expected due to shrinkage of larger mass of melt at the junction. (See figure 25-13). It could be minimised by reducing injection speed at the entry of melt at that position, increasing the injection time and by increasing follow-up pressure. Sink mark can be less influence if the rib thickness is at a certain proportion to the main wall thickness. This proportion will be different for different polymers.

What is the significance of cooling system in the mould?

Traditionally, cooling system is the last area to be considered while designing and building the mould. Too often, cooling system is not even considered until it is too late in the tool design stage to change the mould so that it provides proper temperature control required for the cavity. The quality and productivity of moulded parts also depends on the efficiency of cooling system. Hence due importance should be given to cooling system design: However, now it is possible to carry out the cooling analysis in CAE software like MOLDFLOW and C-Mold. With these software it possible to evaluate the effectiveness and efficiency of cooling system in the mould.

What are the design considerations for cooling system in the mould?

Heat flow takes place from polymer melt to mould steel by

- ❖ effective thermal difusivity of polymer melt and
- ❖ Conduction.

This heat is to be removed by circulating cooling fluid through the cooling channels in core as well as cavity during cooling period in order to maintain the desired temperature.

Uneven temperature of the mould surface results in parts with moulded-instresses, warped sections, sink marks, poor surface appearance and varying part dimensions from cycle to cycle and even cavity to cavity. The temperature control of mould sufrace can be ensured by good design of cooling circuit and cooling system. The mould designer should take care of following points:

- ❖ Cooling system of the mould should have adequate number of cooling channels of suitable size at equal distance from each other and from cavity walls.

- Cooling circuits should be positioned symmetrically around the cavity. There can be sufficient number of independent circuits to ensure uniform temperature along the mould surface.
- The coolant flow rate should be sufficient to provide turbulent flow in the channel.
- There should be no dead ends in the cooling channels. It could provide opportunity for air trap.
- Many a times it is difficult to accommodate cooling channels in the smaller cores or cores with difficult geometry. In such case the core should be made of Beryllium copper which has high thermal conductivity. These core inserts should be located near the cooling channel.
- The seals of coolant system should not leak inspite of application of frequent clamping force and mould expansion/contraction due to thermal cycle during moulding. The O-ring should be positioned so that there is no chance of them being damaged or improperly seated during mould assembly. Seal and O-ring grove should be machined to closely match the contour of the seal. It should ensure that seal is slightly compressed when the mould is assembled.
- There is enough scope for confusion while giving water connection to mould when there are more number of cooling circuits particularly on bigger moulds. A sketch indicating cooling circuits should be available during mould set up.
- Hot runner mould should be provided with compression resistant insulating plates between back plate and machine platen. This is to prevent the heat flow from mould to machine platen, which can create an unbalanced heat flow in the mould. With out insulating plate machine platen will act like a big heat sink, there by destabilising the possible balance between heat given to the mould by the hot melt, and heat taken away by circulating water through mould.

VARIATION IN WALL THICKNESS :

External corner should also have radius to reduce sink mark and stress reduction to improve impact resistance.

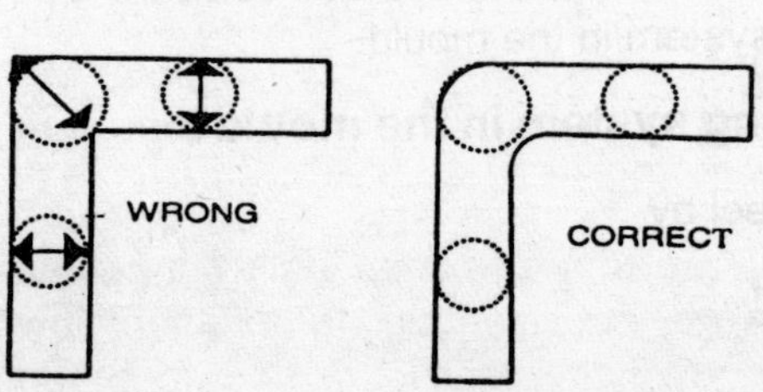

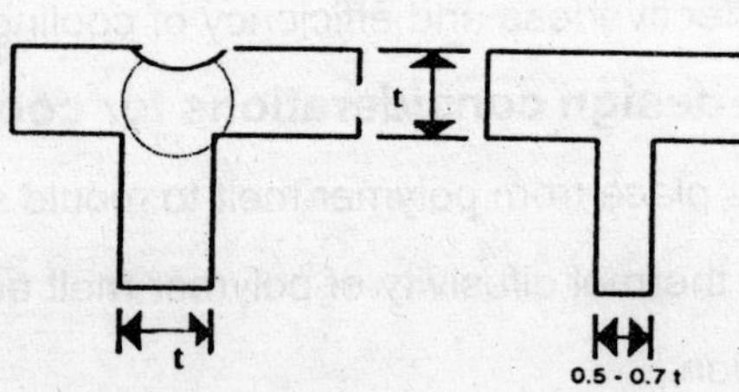

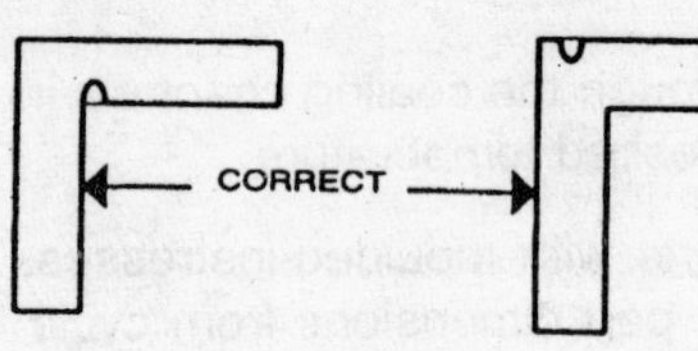

Rib wall thickness should be less than the main wall thickness to avoid sink mark at junction.

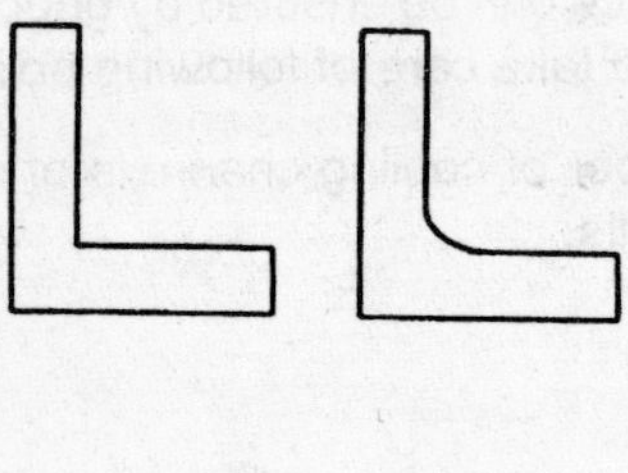

Sharp internal corners act like a notch, through which crack can propagate in the event of high impact. It is recommended to have a radius of 0.5 to 0.6 times wall thickness at the corners.

CONSTANT TEMPERATURE LINE CONTOURS SHOWING TEMPERATURE GRADIENT ACROSS THE MOULD

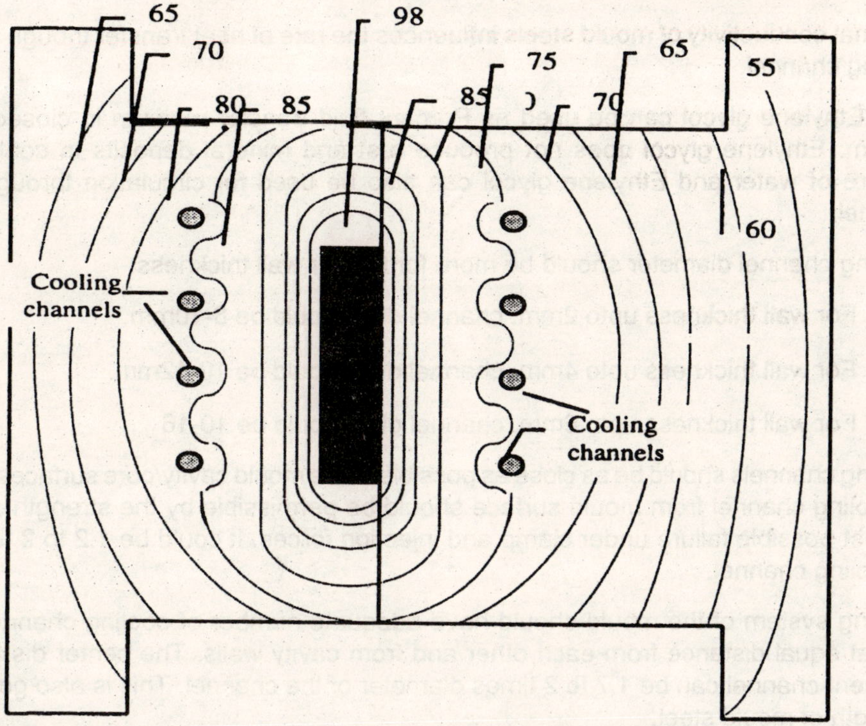

What is the importance of mould temperature control?

Mould temperature control is the most important factor in injection moulding for it influences the moulding quality as well as cycle time and thereby affects production economics. The mould designer, thus, has the important tank, not only to design the mould to be safe and reliable but also to create the **best possible optimised heat transfer conditions so that maximum outputs combined with highest possible quality will be achieved.**

Moulds are usually built with cooling channels. These channels are usually connected in series with one inlet outlet for water flow. The water flow rate may not be enough for turbulent flow because the water pump capacity itself may not be adequate. This obviously leads to random temperature variation on the mould surface. With the result, uncontrolled temperature drift, varying part dimensions and irregular warped surface appears on mouldings.

To produce moulded parts of precise and tolerance, the cavity temperature must be controlled during moulding process. With increasing part quality requirements, tighter dimensional tolerance and reduced rejection rates, Tighter temperature control of mould surface beomes inevitable.

The cooling system is the last area to be considered while designing and building the mould. Too often, cooling is not even considered until it is too late in the tool design stage to change the mould so that it provides proper temperature control required for the cavity. The quality and productivity of moulded parts also depends on the efficiency of cooling system. Hence due importance should be given to cooling system design.

What are factors influencing uniformity of mould surface temperature?

The mould designer should take care of following points:

- ❖ Thermal conductivity of mould steels influences the rate of heat transfer though mould steel to cooling channel.

- ❖ Pure Ethylene glycol can be used as Primary fluid transfer medium in closed loop cooling system. Ethylene glycol does not produce rust and mineral deposits in cooling channels. Mixture of water and Ethylene glycol can also be used for circulation through the cooling channel.

- ❖ Cooling channel diameter should be more for thicker wall thickness:

    - ❖ For wall thickness upto 2mm. channel dia. should be 8-10mm.

    - ❖ For wall thickness upto 4mm. channel dia. should be 10-12mm.

    - ❖ For wall thickness upto 6mm. channel dia. should be 10-16

- ❖ Cooling channels should be as close as possible to the mould cavity/core surfaces. The distance of cooling channel from mould surface should be permissible by the strength of mould steel against possible failure under clamp and injection forces. It could be 1.2 to 2 times diameter of cooling channel.

- ❖ Cooling system of the mould should have adequate number of cooling channels of suitable size at equal distance from each other and from cavity walls. The center distance between adjacent channel can be 1.7 to 2 times diameter of the channel. This is also governed by the strength of mould steel.

- ❖ The difference between the inlet and outlet water temperature should be less than 2 to 5 degrees C. However, for precision moulding, it should be 1 degree C or even 0.5 degree C.

- ❖ Cooling circuits should be positioned symmetrically around the cavity. There can be sufficient number of independent circuits to ensure uniform temperature along the mould surface.

- ❖ The coolant flow rate should be sufficient to provide turbulent flow in the channel.

- ❖ There should be no dead ends in the cooling channels. It could provide opportunity for air trap.

- ❖ Many a times it is difficult to accommodate cooling channels in the smaller cores or cores with difficult geometry. In such case the core should be made of Beryllium copper which has high thermal conductivity. These core inserts should be located near the cooling channel.

- ❖ The seals of coolant system should not leak in-spite of application of frequent clamping force and mould expansion/contraction due to thermal cycle during moulding. The O-ring should be positioned so that there is no chance of them being damaged or improperly seated during mould assembly. Seal and O-ring grove should be machined to closely match the contour of the seal. It should ensure that seal is slightly compressed when the mould is assembled.

- ❖ Mould temperature above 100 degree C normally requires oil as the heating medium. Heat transfer coefficient of oil is lower than that of water.

- ❖ There is enough scope for confusion while giving water connection to mould when there are more number of cooling circuits particularly on bigger moulds. A sketch indicating cooling circuits should be available during mould set up.

- Hot runner mould should be provided with compression resistant insulating plates between back plate and machine platen. This is to prevent the heat flow from mould to machine platen, which can create an unbalanced heat flow in the mould. With out insulating plate machine platen will act like a big heat sink, there by destabilising the possible balance between heat given to the mould by the hot melt, and heat taken away by circulating water through mould.
- The cooling channel layout is suitable when the isothermal i.e. the equipotential lines, are at a constant distance from surface of the mouldings. This ensures that heat flow density is same everywhere.
- Provision for thermocouple fixing should be available at specific one or two places in core as well as caivity to monitor the temperature of mould.
- Use efficient sealing methods and materials to eliminate cooling leaks.
- Poor mould surface temperature control can cause following quality problems:
    - Axial eccentricity, Radial eccentricity, Angular deviation, Warpage, Surface defects, Flow lines.

STABILISATION OF MOULD SURFACE TEMPERATURE

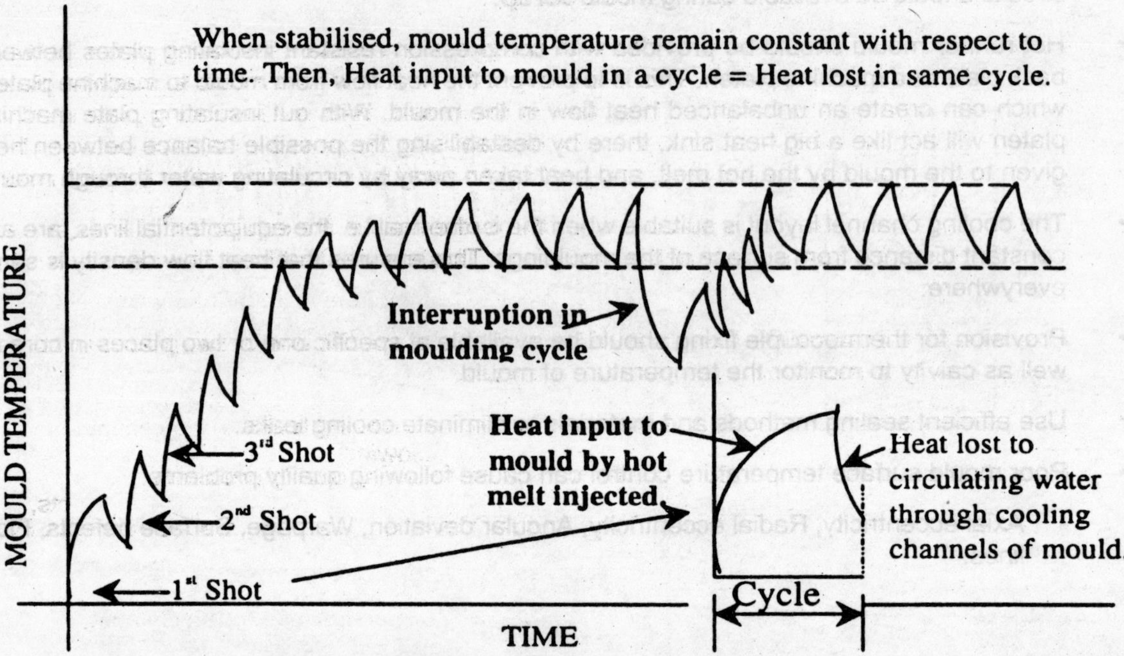

How does heat exchange take place in the injection mould?

To obtain uniform mould surface temperature control, the cooling system must be designed to remove the heat from the melt as it enters the mould. It must also provide rapid cooling of the part so that a repetitive and economical cycle can be obtained.

The speed of heat exchange between the injected plastic melt and the mould is an important factor in speeding up the moulding cycle - productivity. Heat has to be taken away from the thermoplastic melt until a stable and balanced condition has been reached to permit demoulding - ejection. The time available to do this balancing of heat exchange is during the cooling period.

The amount of heat to be carried away depends on

melt temperature.
demoulding - ejection temperature and
specific heat of plastic melt.

For thermosets and elastomers heat has to be supplied to injected material to initiate curing.

VARIATION OF TEMPERATURE AT DIFFERENT POINTS OF THE MOULD AS A FUNCTION OF TIME

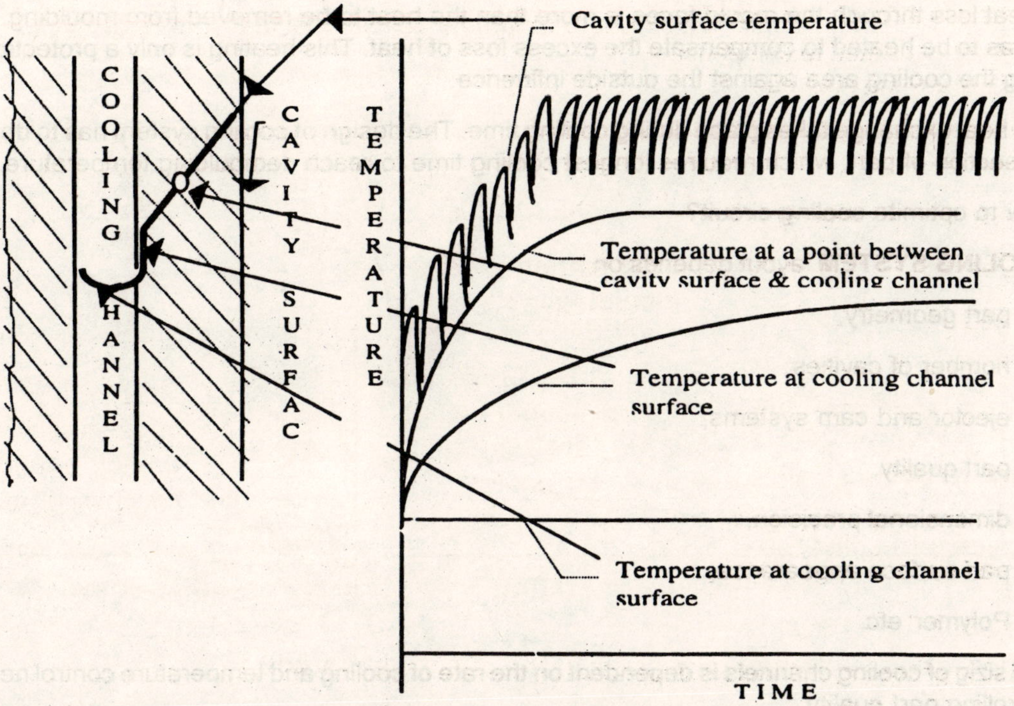

HEAT EXCHANGE IN INJECTION MOULD: (Figure 25- 17)

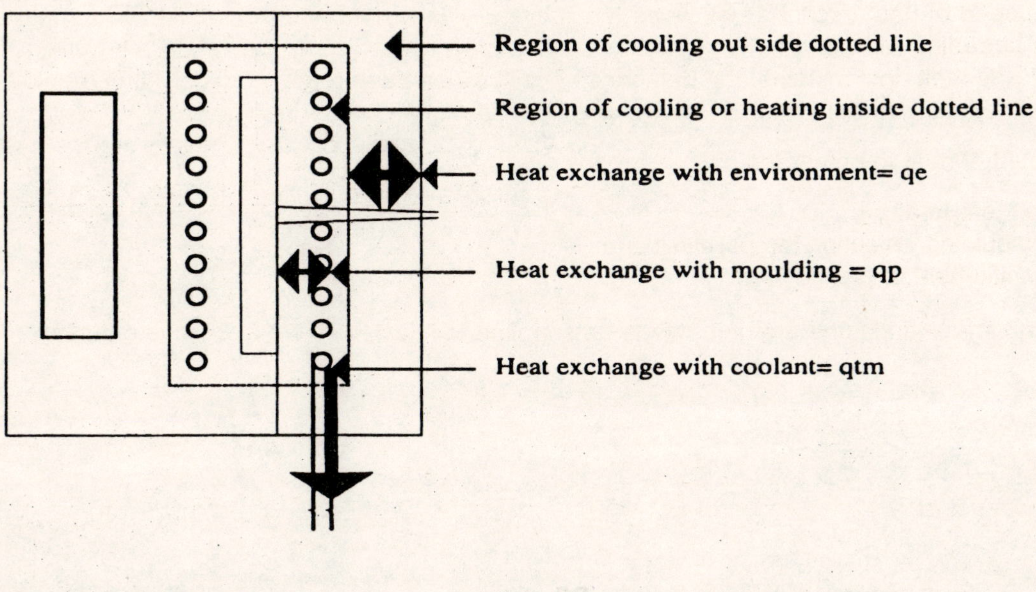

When the mould is required to be heated during production run?

The mould has to be heated or cooled depending on the temperature outside mould surface and that of environment.

If heat loss through the mould faces is more than the heat to be removed from moulding. then mould has to be heated to compensate the excess loss of heat. This heating is only a protection for shielding the cooling area against the outside influence.

The heat exchange takes place during cooling time. The design of cooling system has to depend on that section of part, which requires longest cooling time to reach demoulding temperature.

How to optimite cooling circuit?

COOLING SYSTEM layout depends on :

- part geometry,
- number of cavities,
- ejector and cam systems,
- part quality,
- dimensional precision,
- part surface appearance,
- Polymer etc.

The sizig of cooling channels is dependent on the rate of cooling and temperature control needed for controlling part quality.

CAE software like **MOLDFLOW** or **C-Mold** can be used to determine the optimised dimension of cooling channel and distance from mould surface, distance between cooling channel, flow rate.

COOLING SYSTEM IN MOULDS - DESIGN

Heat removal from core of less than 3mm. by air when mould opens. Continuous cooling may not be practical.

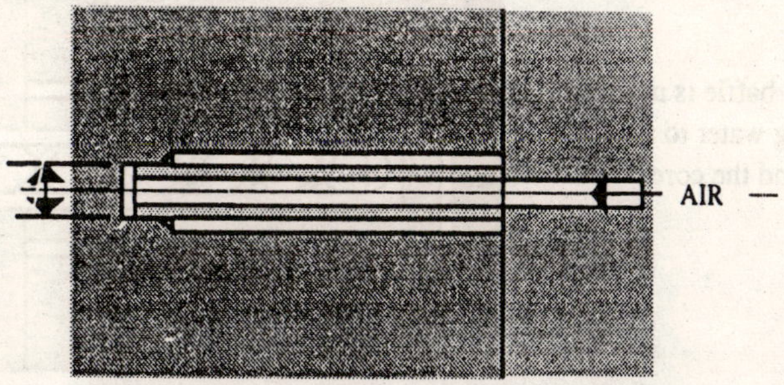

Heat conducting copper is connected to cooling line for core diameter less than 5mm. Base of insert should be enlarged.

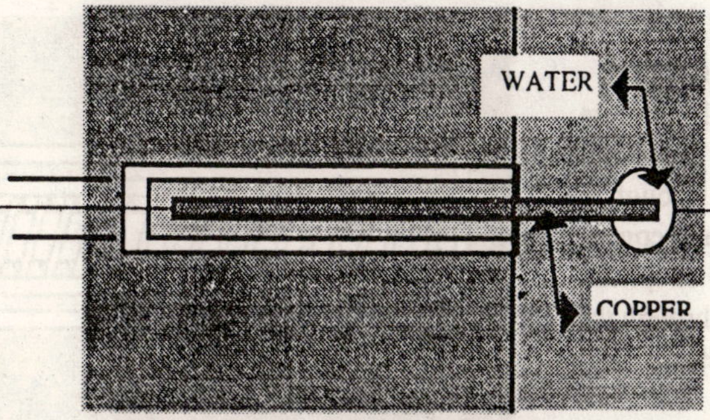

Bubbler with tip beveled for core diameter. of less than 8 mm..

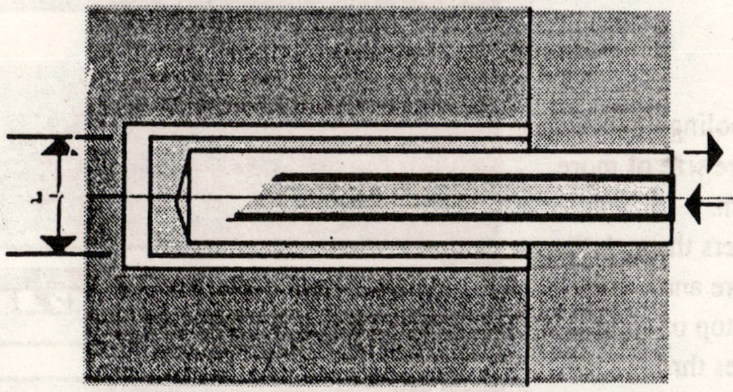

Baffle used as partition in cooling channel for directing water all around core.

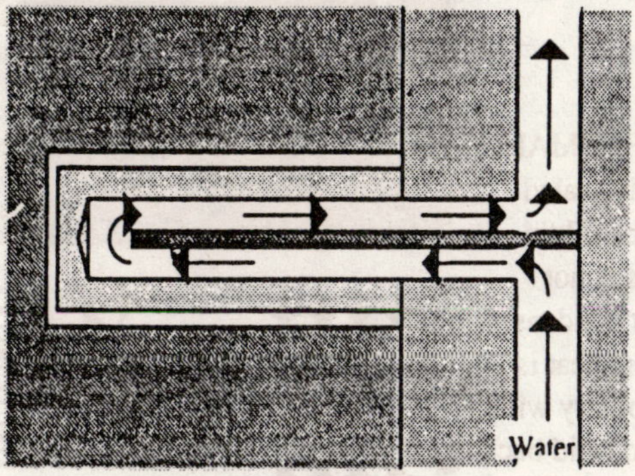

Twisted baffle is used for directing water to flow all around the core.

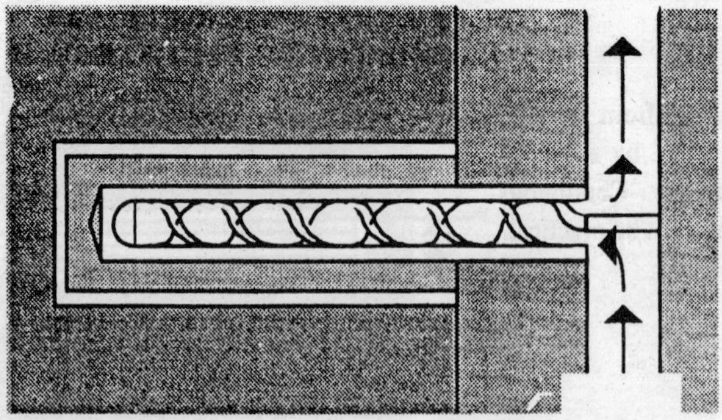

Spiral core,- single or double spiral - for core diameter of 12 to 50mm. Water enters through the central bore and comes out at the top of spiral. It circulates through the spiral channel and returns to outlet.

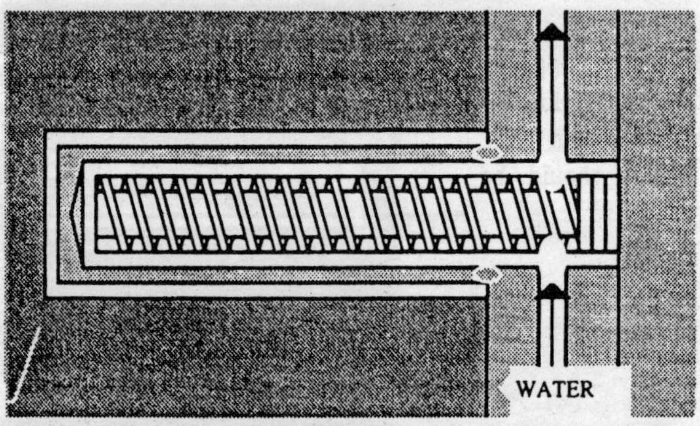

Helical cooling channels are for core size of more than 40mm. Water enters through the central bore and comes out at the top of spiral. It circulates through the spiral channel and returns to outlet.

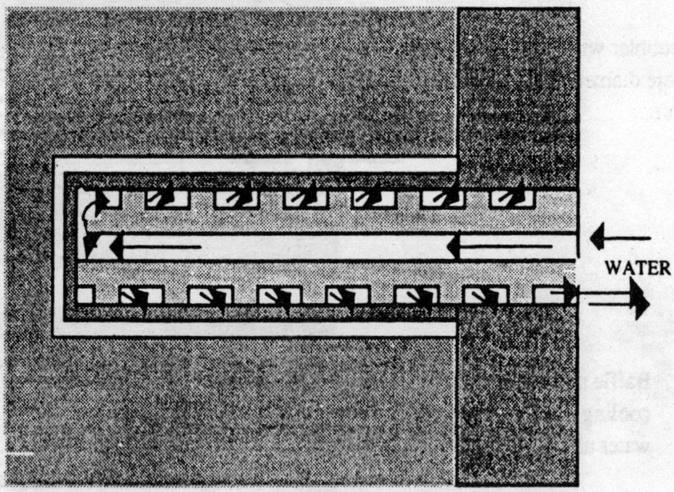

HEAT PIPE / THERMAL PIN: Hermetically sealed stainless steel tube. Fluid inside evaporates at hot point and vapour condenses at other end where heat is dissipated. A capillary wick passes condensed fluid back to hotspot

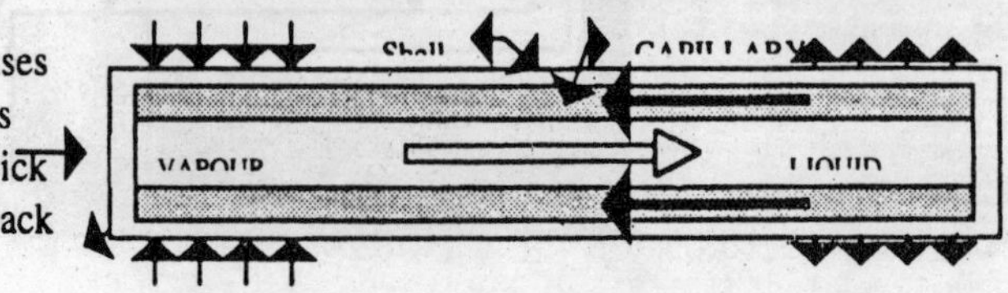

CORE COOLING IN SERIES

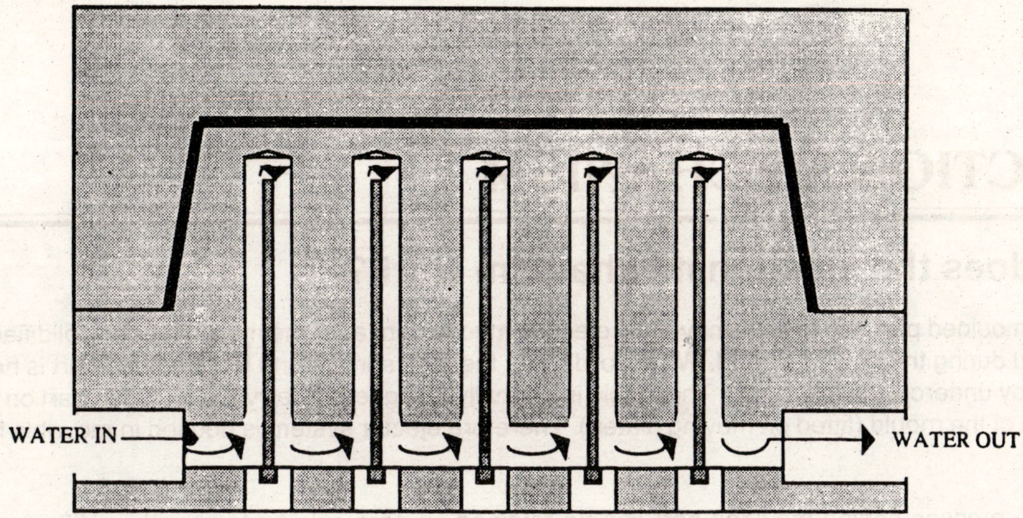

PARALLEL LAYOUT OF BUBBLER COOLING: (Figure 25-20)

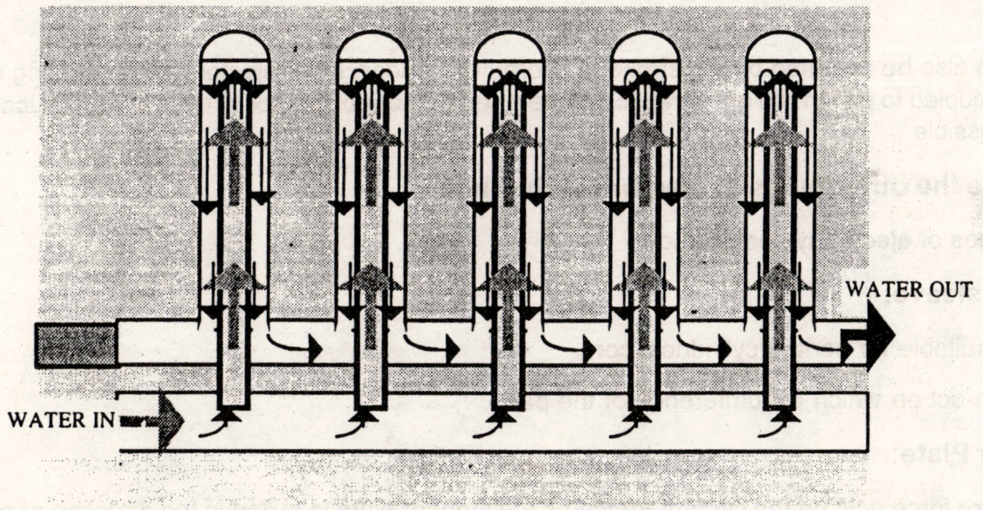

COOLING SYSTEM FOR FLAT PARTS

Sprial Cooling is more preferred as it is more efficient straight line cooling. Inefficient cooling would lead to warping (wavy surface) of large flat area. See figure 18.06 for cooling system for flat rectangular part and figure 18.07 for flat round part. Also refer figure 18.08 for flat rectangular part with center gate.

4

EJECTION MECHANISM

How does the ejection mechanism work?

The moulded part has to be removed by ejection mechanism after the melt has been solidified in the mould during the cooling period. While solidifying, the melt shrinks and the moulded part is held/ retained by undercuts in the mould. The mould is normally designed to carry the moulded part on the core side of the mould (fiffed on moving platen). Therefore ejector system is housed in movable half of mould.

While process setting moulded part can be retained on core side by temperature differences between core & cavity. In this core force required for ejection is quite high.

The ejection mechanism is normally actuated mechanically during mould open stroke. Ejector system includes number of ejector pins mounted on ejector plate. It pushes the moulded part off the core. While mould opens, ejector plate hits a fixed bolt on the machine, which actuates the ejector system.

It can also be actuated by the stroke of hydraulic cylinder. If the ejector rod connecting ejector plate is coupled to piston rod of hydraulic cylinder then number of ejector strokes in rapid succession is also possible.

What are the other types of ejector mechanism?

Other types of ejector system includes

Ejector sleeve:

It is suitable for central cylindrical core.

It can act on which circumference of the part.

Stripper Plate:

Ejector force acts on the circumference as the stripper plate is pulled in the direction of ejection with a stripper bolt or it could be actuated by hydraulic cylinder.

Double Stage Ejection :

The ejection by small hydraulic cylinder (in the mould) releases the moulded part from the core and further ejection is carried out by stripper plate which is pushed by ejector and rod mounted on ejector plate.

Combined Ejection with Compressed Air :

During mould open stroke moulded part is stripped off the core mechanically, and final ejection is done with compressed air.

Ejection in Three Plate Mould:

In three plates moulds the mould open at the runner systems first and then thereafter at the parting line of moulded part. The ejector system by stripper bolt opens the parting at runner first and then it opens at moulded part. The runner system is held by an under cut until it is ejected by an ejector bar actuated by a bolt.

Similar sequence can also be possible by latch mechanism. While mould open latch is on, the parting line at runner system opens first. The latch is then lifted by a cam as mould opens further thereby releasing the latch and parting-line-at-moulded part opens.

Reversed Ejection from Stationary side:

If core is on the stationary platen then the ejector mechanism consists of stripper plate and stripper plate is used for ejection of moulded part.

Ejection of part with under cuts:

Demoulding parts with undercuts by slipping them off without eliminating the undercuts in the mould is possible only if the moulded part can be sufficiently deformed to overcome the undercut. The deformation caused by the under cut must not be greater than the deformation at the elastic limit of the plastic melt.

Threaded parts of low modules of elasticity of PA6, PP, PE can be stripped off the core if they have suitable thread. (Other depth less than 0.3mm).

A collapsible core is used for demoulding internal thread.

Interchangeable cores can be used for demoulding internal threaded moulded part.

Unscrewing arrangement :

The cores for internal threaded part or sleeve for external threaded parts can be rotated in the mould during mould open and close movement. The linear open/close movement can be converted to rotation by rack & pinion arrangement on the mould. The rotation of the pinion is transferred to cores in multi cavity mould again by gear of each core and a rack.

External drive of hydraulic or pneumatic motor can also be used.

If the moulded part has external under cut then during demoulding slides are positively actuated by leader pins or cams. Leaders pin or cam are at an angle pull the sliding block as the mould open thereby releasing the moulded part from the under cut portion.

In the spilt cavity mould the cavity is split in two wedges shaped sliding blocks. They are guided in a frame by a cam arrangement. Slides are led in dovetail shaped groove as mould closes and slides separate as mould opens.

What is Core-Pull mechanism? How does it work?

The parts like pipefittings require core movement side wise i.e. perpendicular to the direction of mould open. If the length of core is such that is can not be moved out by length of leader pin or cams then the core has to be moved out by hydraulic cylinder of adequate stroke.

There can be more than one core depending on the part geometry. The cores may or may not move simultaneously. If the all the cores move simultaneously then one hydraulic circuit can operate all the cores by connecting their respective hydraulic cylinders in parallel. In this case mono block distributor accommodating HP hose connection to the required number of cylinders would be necessary.

If the cores are required to move at different instants then independent hydraulic circuits for core pull are required. Each hydraulic circuit includes pressure reducing valve, flow control valve, directional valve and monoblock distributor for HP hose connections. The hydraulic cylinders are part of the mould and therefore it can be the part of machine.

The user or mould maker should specify the core pull sequence and requirement of number of hydraulic circuit for a given mould. Mould maker should also specify the requirements limit switches in the core pull sequence. Core-pull sequence can be programmed on the card as per the requirement of the mould.

What is the possible core pull sequences?

Normally, cores may be required to be pulled-in

- ❖ before mould close commences,
- ❖ during mould close operation (simultaneously),
- ❖ at any point defined by a limit switch on the mould close stroke. Mould may be required to stop movement till core pull-in is over, at the end of mould close stroke and before mould clamp.

Cores may be required to be pulled-out

- ❖ after decompression of clamp tonnage and before mould open commences,
- ❖ during mould open operation,
- ❖ at any point defined by a limit switch on the mould open stroke. Mould may be required to stop movement till core pull-out is over,
- ❖ at the end of mould open stroke and before ejection.

It is required to ensure that cores are in right position before the two halves of the mould touch each other or before the commencement of clamp force or even before the mould start moving (open/close). For this purpose there can be limit switches on the mould.

What facilitates release of part from the mould during ejection?

Release performance of moulded product depends on

- ❖ mould quality - high degree of polishing is desired
- ❖ part geometry - slight taper and proper designing of under cut.

- polymer
- processing condition - over packing should be watched.

A part with intricate geometry with thinner wall thickness and insert should be filled at correct melt viscosity. Slight decrease in melt viscosity will result in over packing. This will result in mould sticking. Hence, melt temperature, mould temperature, injection speed, injection pressure should have very precise control.

- Mould release agents like zinc sterate and silicon sprays are available.
- Mould release can be improved by
- decreasing mould temperature
- increasing cooling time
- reducing injection/flow up pressure
- improving mould surface finish

BASIC STEPS FOR MOULD DESIGN

	ORDER FOR MOULD	
DETAILS OF ORDER	Size or order, costs, delivery dates.	
PART	Part geometry, material, appearance, tolerance, strength, and other	
	properties test methods.	
MACHINE DATA		
	MOULD DESIGN	
	BASIC PROCEDURE FOR MOULD DESIGN.	
1.	Number of cavities.	
2.	Cavity layout.	
3.	Number of parting lines.	
4.	Dimension of cavity.	
5.	Sprue & runner	
6.	Gates.	
7. 8.	Cooling system. Mechanical design. Strength of steel, Thermal conductivity for heat exchange system, Thermal expansion for tolerance, Coefficient of friction for rubbing parts, Abrasion resistance & corrosion resistance for melt flow.	
9.	Core movement system	

10.	Hydraulic cylinders	
11.	Exact cavity dimension.	
12.	Ejector system.	
13.	Alignment system.	
14.	Venting.	
15.	Mounting options.	
16.	Core movement system	
17.	Hydraulic cyulinders	
18..	Selection of steels	
19.	Fabrication of mould	

CHECK LIST FOR A TURNKEY MOULD PROJECT

A	PART DRAWING	FIXED MOULD HALF	MOVING MOULD HALF	COMMENT
	Unity of part understood.			Service condition. Based on properties
	Material selected.			Based on properties
	Shrinkage calculated correct			Based on data & experience
	Gate type & location selected; and is acceptable.			For balanced flow or unbalanced flow
	Runner sized for balanced flow.			For balanced flow.
	Parting line acceptable.			Esthetic/functional
	Possible weld line & its strength debated.			Shift to less critical area.
	Possible sink marks acceptable.			Part design problem
	Matching contours for assembly.			Workmanship.
	Tolerance attainable.			Deep study
	Decorating requirement noted.			

	Inspection equipment noted.			
	Cooling fixtures required			
	Assembly operation required.			
	Draft and part finish noted.			
	Quality Level requirements.			
	Hydraulic cylinders for core pull			
	LS installation on mould.			
	Selection of steels.			
		Available on machine	Estimated for process	
B	**INJECTION MOULDING MACHINE**			
	Make and Model			
	Clamp force & Toggle/ hydraulic ram.			Max - day light & open stroke
	Platen size			To suit mould mounting.
	Clearance between tie bars			To accomodate mould.
	Minimum mould height			Shut mould Height be more
	Mould open stroke.			More than 2 times part depth.
	Max. Ejector stroke & force.			More than part depth.
	Locating ring size			To confirm.
	Screw diameter/ maximum swept Volume			Max-shot weight should be more than actual shot wt.
	Maximum injection rate			To spread melt before freeze

	Maximum injection pressure			Sufficient for pack melts.
	Plasticising rate			Adequate to doze with in optimum cooling time
	Screw rpm.			
	Barrel tenmperature profile			
	Back pressure			
	Recovery time			With in cooling time.
	Suck back required.			
	Nozzle type			
	Nozzle contact radius.			
	Sprue bush matching Nozzle			
	Ejection			
	Ejector release/coupling			
	Water connection.			
	Heater connections.			
	Air connections			
	Core pull connections.			
	Limit switches			
	Regrind allowed.			

C	**MOULD DETAILS** Type			
	Dimensions			To match machine platen
	Daylight required			To match machine
	Selection of steels for varrious mould components.			
	Sprue bush radius diameter.			To confirm

	Parting line efficient.			Workman ship of mould.
	Runner system dimensions finalised			**For balanced flow**
	Type of Gates finalised. 15 degree relief.			**For balanced flow**
	Sprue puller to ensure part remains on core on mould open.			
	Guide pins, cam pins oversized in diameter and supported by thicker plates.			It should have sufficient length to enter other half before entry of longest core
	Thickness plates to withstand excess forces and deformations.			Additional Cost of thicker plate is negligible. It improves life of mould.
	Cavity layout finalised			
	Core & Cavity designed for ease of fabrication. Correct shrinkage is considered.			**To withstand high cavity pressure.**
	Exposure to side thrust noted.			**Backed with solid steel.**
	Large slides provided with grease grooves.			
	Slides acting against gravity are provided with spring.			
	Heat treatment noted.			Based on hardness needs
	Venting noted.			
	Cavity finish noted.			
	Draft.			For ease of part release
	Cavity Cooling circuits.			Uniform surface temp.
	Special cores for heat removal.			No space for cooling hole.
	Cores Cooling circuits mechanical			**Uniform surface temp.**

	Adequate Ejector pins and size			for balanced ejection with out deformation.
	Ejector stroke dimensioned.			To verify machine spec.
	Ejector rod to be strong enough			
	Ejector sequence			
	Core pull - Hydraulic			
	Core pull Sequence			
	LS/Proxy Switches mounted			
	Cavities numbered.			
	Material to be used for Moulding			
	Shrinkage.			
	Tolerance anticipated.			
	Thermocouple in mould			
	Uniform texture			
	Insert required.			
	Tapped holes for lifting and shipping straps provided.			
D	**HOT RUNNER TYPE** Heat capacity.			
	Gate type.			
	No. of plugs.			
	Electrical load.			
	No. of thermocouple.			
	Temperature setting.			

E	**UNSCREWING**			
	MOULD.			
	Method/			

	Mechanical			
	Electrical			
	Hydraulic			
	Air.			
	Internal/external to mould.			
	Core stripper plate travel.			
	COMMENTS			

INJECTION MOULD SPECIFICATION SHEET

CUSTOMER	**CONTACT**	**DATE**
PART	**PHONE NO.**	
DRG. NO.	**MOULD NO:**	
SMATERIAL		

MOULD TYPE		**CAVITIES**		**RUNNERS**	
2 Plate		Number		Full round.	
3 plate		Balanced		Semi round	
Hot runner		Unbalanced		Quater round	
Surface area		Inserted		Trapeziodal	
Production life				U shaped	
Parts per year.				Cold slug	

GATING		Ring	
Sprue inside/out side		Disc	
Film		Full edge	
Submarine		Spider	
Tab		Pin point	
Pin		Degating type	
Fan		hot runner	
COOLING SYSTEM			
Optimum coolin		Turbulent cooling	
Cooled cores		Water line diameter	
Cooled core pins		in core	
Each cavity separates		in cavity	
Cooled cavity plate		in cores	
Individual circuit		Water connections type	
Surge cooling			
HEATING SYSTEM			
Hot water			
Hot oil			
Catridge heater watts			
in core			
in cavity			

WORK SHEET FOR SELECTION OF STEEL FOR MOULD

	P-20	H-13	A-2	D-2	420 SS	P-6	0-1	S-7	BER-CU	SIL BRN	CASE HARDENED	HARDENED	QUENCHED	TEMPERED	NITRIDED	CROMED
CAVITY PLATES																
CAVITY INSERTS																
CORE PLATE-																
CORE INSERTS																
SLIDERS																
BACK UP PLATES																
EJECTOR PLATE																
GUIDE PINS																
BUSHES																

TYPES OF DEMOULDING

Demoulding		Unscrewing timed by	
Stripper plate		Hydraulic/air/ mechanical	
Round ejectors		Sprue puller plate	
Stripper sleeves		Slide	
Two stage strip		Slide	
Flat ejector		Sprue puller type	
Angled			

TYPE OF FINISH

CAVITY SURFACE	**DRAFT**	**ON CORE**	**ON CAVITY**		
FINISH	**ON CAVITY**	**.ON CAVITY**	**FINISH**	**ON CAVITY**	**ON CAVITY**
High polish			Sand blasted		
Polish			EDM		
Polish one dorection			Chrome plated		
Ground			Textured type & depth		
Wet honed					
FINISH QUALITY			Parting line match		
on moving			on moving cores		

VENTING			
Cavity		Dead pockets	
Core		Dummy pin	

Ejector pins		Vacuums venting	
Blind vents		Vent blow back	

MISCELLANEOUS				
Temperature sensors		Decoration required		
Pressure sensors		Drawing available		
Dial gauge		Insulated plate		
Mould number		Sprue		
Cavity numbered		Locating ring		
Engraving - raised / undercut		Standard mould parts		
Templates supplied		Special mould parts.		

MACHINE SPECIFICATIONS RECOMMENDED

MACHINE SPECIFICATIONS RECOMMENDED.		**SELECTED MACHINE**
CLAMP FORCE	More than	
PLATEN SIZE	More than	
TIE BAR CLEARANCE	More than	
MAX-DAY LIGHT	More than	
MIN. MOULD HEIGHT	More than	
MAX OPEN STROKE	More than	
EJECTOR STROKE MAX.	More than	
MAX EJECTOR FORCE	More than	
MAX. SWEPT VOLUME	More than	
SCREW DIA/STROKE	More than	
MAX INJECTION RATE	More than	

MAX INJECTION PRESSURE	More than	
MAX PLASTICISING RATE	More than	
ADDITIONAL CONTROLS FOR HOT RUNNERS CORE PULL		

QUALITYCHECK LIST

PART QUALITY SPECIFIED	DESIRED	ACHIEVED	REMARKS
MATERIAL-GRADE			
COLOUR			
SURFACE FINISH			
WELD LINE			
SINK MARKS			
DROP TEST			
LOAD TEST			
IMPACT TEST			

5

PRODUCTION SCHEDULE OF PLASTIC INJECTION MOULD

PRODUCTION SCHEDULE OF PLASTIC INJECTION MOULD															
PART NAME:															
PART NO.															
ESTIMATED WEEKS FOR COMPLITION															
START WEEK															
COMPLITION WEEK															
TESTING WEEK															
DELIVERY WEEK															
		PERCENTAGE COMPLITION/CALENDAR WEEKS													
		1	2	3	4	5	6	7	8	9	10	11	12	13	14
ACTIVITIES ES	%														
BACK PLATES															
PREPARATIONS															
Squate/ build up		100													
lift holes		100													
Water lines						50	50	55	55	55	55	55	55	55	100
Rough machine		10	15	20	40	80	100								
CAVITY INSERTS															
Square plates		50	85	100											
Rough machine					0	80	100								
Finish machine						10	50	100							
Water lines								50	50	55	55	55	55	55	100

EDM															
Electrode prearation				10	25	50	75	88	90	99	100				
Machining with EDM												30	60	100	
Stone													40	80	100
EJECTOR															
BASE PREPARATION															

Square/ build up		100													
lift holes		100													
Water lines									80	90	95	95	95	95	100
Insert pokect			20	30	40	50	60	80	100						
Rough machine															
CORE INSERT															
Square plates		100													
Rough machine		50	60	75	80	100									
finish machine						10	40	50	55	60	70	80	90	100	
EDM															
Electrode preparation								50	90	90	100				
Machining with EDM												100			
Stone															100
Heat treatment															
EJECTOR SYSTEM															
Build up and fit			70	80	80	85	85	100							
FINAL ASSEMBLY															
runner & gates												100			
Fit & assembly												100			
Assembly															
Vents															
TRIALS															
Trial #1															
Fit & Adjestment															
Trial #2															
Fit & adjestment															

Final inspection															
Texture															
Trial-final															
First sample															
TOTAL MOULD	100														

DETAILS OF JOB-ORDER FOR MOULDING SHOP

NEW ORDER FOR MOULDING SHOP

MATERIAL		**PART DETAILS**	
PART NAME		OVER ALL SIZE	
MATERIAL		**WALL THICKNESS**	
GRADE		MINIMUM mm	
COLOUR		MAXIMUM mm.	
HEAT DEFL TEMP.		MOST PREVAILING mm.	
RECO. MELT TEMP.		FLOW RATIO	
MFI		- MAXIMUM	
DENSITY AT 250 C		PROJECTED AREA sq. cm.	
PREHEAT TEMP.			
PREHEAT TIME			
THERMAL			
STABILITY			
SHRINKAGE			
MOULD DETAILS			
MOULD TYPE	2 PLATE/3 PLATE /STRIPPER PLATE	EJECTOR TYPE	PINS/SLEEVE/STRIPPER PLATE/ UNSCREWING
MOULD SIZE		EJECTOR STROKE	
LOCATING RING		EJECTOR COUPLING	AVAILABLE/TO BE MADE
HOOK SIZE		EJECTION	SINGLE STAGE/DOUBLE STAGE/ AIR ASSISTED
NO. OF CAVITIES		REVERSED EJECTION	

RUNNER SYSTEM		AIR EJECTION	
HOT RUNNER		NO. OF AIR NOZZLE	
INSUL. RUNNER		NO. OF CKD.	
GATE. TYPE		SEQUENCE	
STEEL		CORE PULL	
CORE		NO OF CYLRS.	
CAVITY		NO. OF CKT.	
PLATES		CORE PULL SEQUENCE	
COOLING			
CORE			
CAVITY		**MACHINE RECOMMENDED** MOULDED ON M/C PAST	
		PAST CYCLE TIME	
NOZZLE TYPE BORE SIZE		NOZZLE SIZE TIP RADIUS	
HEATER REQ.			
REMARK:			

6

STEEL FOR INJECTION MOULD

What are the factors to be considered while selecting steel for injection mould?

To design and build a high quality mould, which is required to consistently produce quality parts, high quality steels must be selected. Steels with the metallurgical characteristics that ensure reliable mould performance, increase safety factor and boost productivity.

While selecting steel for Injection mould one must consider the following points:

- What clamp force machine - higher clamp force machine - will be used?
- What polymer is being considered for moulding?
- What is pressure in cavity?
- What is the production quantity expected from mould?
- What is the %age of steel cost of mould?
- What are wearing resistance, toughness and relationship between them?

In injection moulding process, Injection pressure maximum up to 2400 kg/sq.cm is encountered. This pressure depends on polymer melt viscosity and maximum flow ratio of part. The peak pressure in cavity acting on projected area is opposed by clamp force. The peak pressure could be 40 - 50% of injection pressure at screw tip.

Usage of much larger clamp force than required is quite common. The application of excessive clamp force can result in excessive deformation of the plates and mould parts. This can reduce useful life of the mould. *Therefore, never under design the mould.*

Requirement of clamp force increases if maximum injection rate of the machine is not adequate.

The cost of steel is approximately 10% of cost of mould. Hence one should not hesitate to increase plate thickness and guide pin/cam pin thickness.

What are the essential characteristics desired in mould steel?

Essential characteristics of Injection Mould Steel:

- Uniform structure and freedom from internal defets.
- Machinability.

- Maximum freedom from distortion during heat treatment.
- Weldability.
- Polishability.
- Wear resistance and toughness

No one steel can have the ideal combination of properties for every application. It is known that all plastic moulds can be made from a relatively small variety of steels.

Steels for mould falls into two categories.

- Structural sections of the mould (mould based & plates).
- Cavities and cores

For the mould base there are two major types of steel used in the majority of standard mould bases.

Medium carbon silicon-kills forging quality steel with approximately 25% greater tensile strength than typical low carbon steel. It is annealed to approx, 165Bhmm. It is stress relieved for minimum deformation during machining.

AISI 4130 type alloy steel is supplied pre-heat treated to approx. 300 Bhn to withstand the peening effects of flash. *It has a durability for heavy compression loads and long production runs. It is also free machining steel, ideal for holder blocks, which require pocket machining, and inserts.*

Wear resistance :

The ability to withstand wear from friction of hot melt and abrasive fillers is a function of steel's hardness. High hardness is obtained from heat treatable, highly alloyed grades. As hardness increases, toughness reduces.

Toughness:

Toughness is the key to a mould's ability to withstand impact, flexing and other stresses with out cracking. To get high toughness, some hardness and some wear resistance usually must be sacrificed. Nitriding or carburising can provide hard surface over tough but softer core.

Machinability:

Ease of machining is baiscally economic consideration. Machinability(metal cutting/grinding) varies inversely with the hardness and alloy content of steel. With electric discharge machining, the metal removal rate is not dependent on steel hardness.

Dimensional stability:

Unless steel is used in prehardened condition, it must be treated or surface hardened to develop adequate hardness. Often these results in a significant change in the cavity dimensions, necessitating finish machining and/or grinding to restore size. Besides the extra cost and time, theses post treattreating steps always pose the risk of stress cracking the mould. Mold steels vary considerably in heat-stability.

NOMINAL CHEMISTRIES FOR PLASTIC MOULD STEELS

AISI Steel		C	Mn	Si	Cr	Ni	Mo	V	W	S
P6	Carburising	0.10	0.50		1.50	3.25				
01	Oil hardening	0.90	1.00		0.50				0.50	
P20	Pre Hardened	0.30	0.90	0.50	1.60		0.25			
S7	Air Hardening	0.50	0.70	0.25	3.25		1.40			
H13	Air Hardening	0.40	0.40	1.10	5.00		1.35	1.10		
A2	Air Hardening	1.00	0.70	0.30	5.25		1.15	0.30		
D2	Air Hardening	1.55			11.5		0.80	0.90		
4240	Pre Hardened	0.40	0.90	0.30	1.00		0.20			0.80
4145	Pre Hardened	0.45	0.90	0.30	1.00		0.20			
TYPE 414	Stainless	0.30	1.00	1.00	12.0	2.00				
TYPE 420	Stainless	0.35	0.40	1.00	13.0					
TYPE 440	Stainless	1.05	1.00	1.00	17.0		0.75			

Lately we have seen the use of a chromium alloyed stainless holder steel (AISI 420F) supplied in a hardened and tempered condition. This has lower mould maintenance cost, due to very low corrosion from the plastic material, and lower production costs since water cooling channels are unaffected by corrosion ensuring a constant cycle time.

What are the factors to be considered while selecting steel for core and cavity?

The prime factor to be taken into account in the selection of the steel for the cavity and core of a mould are as follows:

- The finish required on the plastic part could vary from a utility finish on the back of the plastics part, to an optical finish for a lens.
- The properties of the plastic material are to be moulded. Most materials have little adverse effect on the steel, G.P. Polystyrene for example. Some are corrosive like most of the vinyl and some materials such as glass-filled resins are extremely abrasive.

- The method of manufacturing of the cavity and core. Certain mould steels are more suitable foe conventional machining and others for E.D.M and hobbing.
- The quanity of plastics part to be produced. More specifically this refers to number of shorts/ cavity the mould has to produce in its lifetime.

What steel is recommended for core & Cavity?

- P-20 is a cavity steel pre-heat treated to approx, 300Bhn. It is produced by electric furnace vacuum degass and is electtricslag remelt. This results in pure steel that has exceptional polishability.
- H-13 is a thermal-shock resistant hot work die steel. It is electric furnace melted, vacuum desgassed and high density forged. It is supplied in fully annealed condition (200 Bhn) Which can be subsequently heat treated to your desired hardness.
- S-7 is achrome/molybdenm tool steel developed to produce the combination of high shock resistance and toughness together with an easy machining.
- T-420 is a stainless steel. It is supplied annealed to approximately 220 Bhn., which makes it readily machinable. It is used where you require highly corrosion resistant cavity steel. This steel had excellent polishing characteristics and is also for moulding products with optical finishes.

APPLICATION OF MOULD STEEL

AISI		APPLICATION
P6	CARBURISING	Suitable for cold hobbing & compression moulds Carburised after cold hobbing.
01	OIL HARDENING	Heat-treated to high hardness. Used for small indented moulds where strength is more important than toughness.
P20	PRE HARDENED Prehardened condition- 300 Brinnel	Most popular & versatile mould steel for all sizes of machine cut moulds. No het treatment required. It can be nitrided for reinforced polymer moulding. It can be chrome/nickel-plated to improve corrosion resistance while moulding PVC Parting line/specific area can be flame hardened for localised wear problem. It can be carburised to over 55 Rc. Case depth can be easily controlled. Good polishability.
S7	AIR HARDENING	Suitable for compression mould. It is highly rated for toughness.
H13	AIR HARDENING	Fine combination of toughness and strength. It is toughnest mould steel. It must be heat treated after machining. Maximum hardness Rc 54. Popular for lens moulds or for moulding abrasive materials and for large compression moulds.

		Nitrided to surface hardness of Rc 65-70. Good dimensional stability during heat treatment.
A2	AIR HARDENING	Good dimensional stability during heat treatment. High hardness Rc60 for moulding abrasive materials. Sutable for compression moulds and small injection moulds.
D2	AIR HARDENING	High chromium & high carbon content. High abrasion resistance. Difficult machine. Fear of grinding cracks. Suitable for Small injection and compression moulds.
4240	PRE HARDENED	
4145	PRE HARDENED	Alloy steel. Suitable for Holders, shoes, or core/cavity retainer plate.
TYP E414	STAINLESS	
TYP E420	STAINLESS	Stainless steel suitable for injection and compression moulds. Corrosion resistance. Recommended for moulds for moulding PVC. It has lower thermal conductivity Outstanding dimensional stability in heat treatment. Highly polishable.
TYP E440	STAINLESS	Same as above

What are the mechanical design factors to be considered for injection mould?

❖ **DON'T UNDER DESIGN**

Moulds that are built with inadequate plate thickness crack in service. With each shot of plastics, a mould parts/plates deflect. The greater the deflection, the sooner the fatigue cracking occurs at corners or sharp radii. Since alloyed or hard steel deflect just as much as soft steels under a given load, deflection can be reduced only by increasing thickness. Doubling the thickness halves deflection.

❖ **AVOID LAMINATING**

It does not reduce deflection.

❖ **AVOID SHARP CORNERS**

Sharp corners are stress raisers and too many moulds break for lack of a small radius.

RADIUS TO IMPROVE IZOD IMPACT STRENGTH:

RADIUS AT BASE IN.	IZOD IMPACT STRENGTH. Ft.lbs.
0.002	4
0.010	7
0.020	16
0.040	19
0.080	22
0.125	27
NOTCH FREE	240

❖ **WATER LINES MUST MEET**

Waterlines drilled from opposite sides often do not meet exactly. This causes sharp recesses. Cooling lines should be free from machining marks. Machining marks and sharp corners are stress raisers. All these things leads to failure of mould by cracking.

❖ **MINIMISE SURFACE STRESSES during removal of material.**

The stresses which remains on surface is proportion to the energy used in removing the material.

7

TROUBLE SHOOTING TIPS

PROBLEM	*POSSIBLE CAUSE*	RECOMMENDED CHANGE
Cracking	*Under design*	increase plate thickness.
	Sharp corners	Provide radius.
	Improper support	Support *evenly*.
	Improperly shimmed	Shim *evenly*.
	Improperly heat treated.	Review heat treatment
	Too hard	Lower hardness by raising tempering temperature
	Wrong steel	Review with mould makers.
	Excessive stresses	Stress relieve after repair.
Washing	*Too soft*	Increase hardness by nitriding or carburising
	Excessive stresses	Stress relieve
	Wrong steel	Review with mould makers.
Pitting	*Too soft*	Increase hardness by nitriding or carburising
	Over carburised	Avoid-discuss with heat treater
	Excessive stresses	Stress relieve before diamond polish
Peening	*Too soft*	Increase hardness-flame harden parting line
	Uneven pressure	Adjust moulding condition
Rusting	*Wrong steel*	Use stainless steel of cromeplate
Orange peel	*Overheating in heat treatment*	Discuss with heat treater
	Decarburised surface	Discuss with heat treater
Carburised suface	*Discuss with heat treater*	
	Overpolish	Hand polish Stress relieve before diamond polish.

Cracking of weld	*Lack of preheating*	Preheat
	Lack of post heating	Preheat
	Improper welding rod	Use same chemistry rod
	Carburised surface	Remove carburised surface
	Nitrided surface	Remove nitrided surface
	Welding area not clean	remove throughly all remains of crack or rust.

PROPERTY COMPARISION OF POPULAR MOULD STEEL

Steel	Toughness	Machinability	Distortion in heat treatment	Polishability	Corrosion resistance.
P6	High	Medium	Low	Very good	Poor
01	Medium	High	Low	Good	Poor
P20	High	Medium to high	Low	Very good	Poor
S7	Very high	High	Low	Good	Poor
H13	Very high	Medium to high	Very low	Very good	Fair
A2	Medium	Medium	Very low	Good	Poor
D2	Low	Low	Very low	Fair to good	Poor
4240	Very high	High	Low	Fair to good	Poor
4145	Very high	High	Low	Fair to good	Poor
TYPE414	Very high	Medium	Low	Very good	Very Good
TYPE420	Medium	Medium	Very low	Very good	Good
TYPE 440	Low	Medium	Low	Good	Fair to good

HEAT TREATMENT OF PLASTIC MOULD STEELS

STEEL	Annealing Temp. F'	Hardening Temp. F	Cooling Medium	Tempering Temp. F	Hardness Rc
P6	1525-1575	1450-1500	Air to Oil	350-450	58-61Case
01	1400-1450	1450-1500	Oil	350-500	59-61
P20	1450-1500	1550-1650	Oil	1075-1150	30-36
S7	1500-1550	1700-1750	Air	500-700	52-56
H13	1550-1650	1825-1900	Air	1000-1100	46-52
A2	1550-1650	1700-1800	Air	350-400	59-62
D2	1600-1650	180-1875	Air	900-1000	54-60

4140	1450-1525	1475-1525	Oil	1200-1250	30-36
4145	1450-1525	1475-1525	Oil	1200-1250	30-36
TYPE 414	1200-1300	1500-1600	Air	700-800	30-35
Type 420	1550-1650	1750-1900	Air or Oil	400-750	48-54
Type 440	1550-1600	1850-1950	Air or Oil	300-500	56-61

What is pre-engineered mould based? What are the advantages with standard mould bases?

Many well established companies are producing standard mould bases and other components required for mould.

It is better to select standard mould bases and components in the mould design. This use of pre-engineered standard mould bases and components manufactured from the quality steels and precision machined to close tolerances, makes them interchangeable in the mould. The availability of the components and standard mould bases in vital to the designer and the mould maker. With these parts available, they can be incorporated into the ejection and cooling system of the mould.

How can we ensure good performance from the mould?

Good performance can be obtained from an Injection mould only if you follow these guidelines.

- Ensure mouldable part design.
- Use good mould steel.
- Use good design practice.
- Use good heat treatment.
- Start the mould properly.
- Run the mould properly.

8

PROPERTIES OF PLASTICS

	Material	Injection Moulding Tempetature °C	Injection Moulding Pressure Kg/cm²	Mould linear shrinkage %mm.mm	Specific gravity
POLYETHYLENE AND ETHYLENE COPOLYMERS					
1.	Low density	150-300	560-2100	1.5-5.0	0.92-0.925
2.	Medium density	150-300	560-2100	1.5-5.0	0.926-0.940
3.	High density	150-300	700-1400	2.0-5.0	0.941-0.965
4.	Ethylene ethyl-acrylae copolymer	125-300	560-1400	1.5-3.5	0.93
5.	Ethylene Vinyl acetate copolymer	125-300	560-1400	0.7-1.1	0.925-0.950
POLYPROPYLENES					
1	Unmodified	200-225	700-1400	1.0-2.5	0.902-0.910
2.	Copolymer	200-225	700-1400	0.9-2.0	0.890-0.905
3.	Inert filled	180-225	700-1400	0.5-1.5	1.0-1.3
4.	Glass reinfored	225-275	700-1400	0.4-0.8	1.05-1.24
5.	Impact (Rubber modified)	200-275	1050	1.0-2.5	0.890-0.910
VINYL POLYMERS AND COPOLYMERS					
1.	Rigid	150-210	700-1400	0.1-0.5	1.30-1.45
2.	Flexible unfilled	160-190	560-1750	0.1-0.5 (Varies with Plasticizer)	1.16-1.35
3.	Flexible filled	160-190	560-1750	0.8-3.5	1.3-1.7
4.	Vinyl Butyral Moulding	150-200	700-2100	0.5-2.5	1.65-1.72
5.	Vinyl Formal Moulding Compounds	150-200	700-2100	0.15-0.30	1.2-1.4
6.	Chlorinated Polyvinyl Chloride Compound	190-210	1050-2800	0.3-0.7	1.49-1.58
7.	Vinyl Butyral Moulding Compound Flexible unfilled	125-170	1050-2100		1.05
8.	ABS Modified Vinyl chloride Rigid Flexible	200	560-1750	0.4-1.5	1.35
9.	PP modified vinyl chloride rigid	115-190	560-1120	0.2-0.5	1.28-1.58

Material	Injection Moulding Tempetature °C	Injection Moulding Pressure Kg/cm²	Mould linear shrinkage %mm.mm	Specific gravity
POLYSTYRENE				
1. Unfilled free flowing general purpose heat resistant	160-250	700-2100	0.1-0.6(C) 0.2-0.6(I)	1.04-1.09
2. Impact Resistant, high impact medium impact	175-300	700-2100	0.2-0.6	1.04-1.10
3. Special Heat and Chemical Resistant Type	175-350	700-2100	0.1-0.8	1.20-1.33
4. 20-30% glass filled	225-310	1050-2800	0.1-0.2	1.20-1.33
5. Styrene Acrylonitrile Copolymer Unfilled	190-290	700-2310	0.2-0.7	1.075-1.100
6. 20-30% glass filled	225-290	1050-2800	0.1-0.2	1.20-1.46
STYRENE - BUTADIENE				
Thermoplastic	150-210	1050-2100	0.1-0.5	0.93-1.10
ACRYLICS				
1. Moulding	160-260	700-1400	0.1-0.4(C)	1.17-1.20
2. Impact Acrylic Moulding Compound	200-260	700-1400	0.2-0.8(I)	1.11-1.18
3. MMA (Alphamethyle-Styrene Copolymer)	175-275	700-2100	0.20-0.6	1.09
4. Acrylic Multi-Polymer	200-240	700-1400	0.6-1.0	1.09-1.14
ALLYLIC RESINS AND MONOMERS				
1. DAP Moulding compound glass filled	150-180	140-420	0.2-0.06	1.61-1.78
2. DAL Moulding Compounds				
1) Mineral filled	-	-	0.5-0.7	1.65-1.68
2) Synthetic fiber filled	-		0.9-1.1	1.34-1.39
COMPOUNDED WITH BUTADIENE ACRYLONITRILE COPOLYMERS				
1. Wood flour cotton flock filled	150-180	140-280	0.4-0.9	1.29-1.35
2. Asbestos filled	155-180	140-280	0.4-0.7	1.57-1.65
3. Rag filled	155-180	140-280	0.2-0.4	1.3-1.35
4. Metal filled, (iron, or lead)	140-160	140-350	0.3-0.4	2.0-4.2

	Material	Injection Moulding Tempetature °C	Injection Moulding Pressure Kg/cm²	Mould linear shrinkage %mm.mm	Specific gravity
CELLULOSIC MOULDING COMPOUNDS					
1.	Ethyl Cellulose Moulding Compounds and sheet	180-260	560-2240	0.5-0.9	1.09-1.17
2.	Cellulose Acetate Moulding	170-260	560-2240	0.3-1.0(C) 0.3-0.8(I)	1.22-1.34
3.	Cellulose propionate moulding compound	170-260	560-2240	0.3-0.9(C) 0.3-0.6(I)	1.17-1.24
4.	Cellulose Acetate Butyrate Moulding Compound	170-240	560-2240	0.3-0.9(C) 0.3-0.6(I)	1.17-1.24
	Chlorinated Polyether	210-230	700-1400	0.4-0.6	1.4
	Ionomers	160-275	700-1400	0.3-2.0	0.93-0.96
ACRYLONITRILE-BUTADIENE-STYRENE					
1.	Extrusion Grade	-	-	0.4-0.5	1.02-1.06
2.	High Impact	190-275	560-1750	0.5-0.8	1.01-1.04
3.	High Heat Resistant	260-275	560-1750	0.5-0.8	1.05-1.08
4.	Medium Impact	220-260	560-1750	0.5-0.8	1.04-1.07
5.	Self-extinguishing	190-220	560-1750	0.6-0.8	1.15-1.21
6.	20-40% Glass filled	260-280	1050-2800	0.1-0.2	1.23-1.36
7.	Clear	225-260	700-1400	0.6-0.8	1.07
NYLONS					
1.	Unmodified	260-310	-	0.8-1.5	1.13-1.15
2.	Nucleated	260-310	-	0.7-1.2	1.13-1.16
3.	30-35% g;ass reinforced	260	-	0.5	1.34-1.42
ACETALS					
1.	Homopolymer	190-235	700-1400	2.0-2.5	1.42
2.	Copolymer	185-240	700-1400	2.0-(Avg)	1.42
3.	20% Glass Filled	175-240	700-1400	1.3-2.8	1.56
4.	25% Glass Filled Copolymer	190-240	700-1400	0.2-0.6	1.61
5.	TFE-Fiber Reinforced	185-225	700-1400	2.0-2.5	1.54

Material		Injection Moulding Tempetature ^0C	Injection Moulding Pressure Kg/cm²	Mould linear shrinkage %mm.mm	Specific gravity
FLUROPLASTICS					
1.	Polychlorotrifluoroethylene	260-300	1400-4200	1.0-1.5	2.1-2.2
2.	FEP Fluoroplastic	310-380	350-1400	3.0-6.0	2.12-2.17
3.	Poly Vinylidene Fluoride	225-275	1050-1400	3.0	1.75-1.78
POLYPHENYLENE SULPHIDES					
1.	Unfilled	300-350	350-1050	1.0	1.34
2.	25% Asbestos filled	300-350	700-1400	-	-
3.	40% Glass filled	300-350	700-1400	-	-
	Polysulfone	325-375	1050-1400	0.7	1.24
	Polymethyl Pentene polymer	250-280	560-1400	1.5-3.0	0.83
PHENOL FOLMALDEHYDE AND PHENOLFURFURAL MOULDING COMPOUNDS					
1.	No Filler	135-160	140-280	1.0-1.2	1.25-1.3
2.	Wood flour and cotton flock filled	145-190	140-350	0.4-0.9	1.34-1.45
3.	Asbestos filled	145-190	140-350	0.2-0.9	1.45-2.00
4.	Mica filled	135-175	140-350	0.2-0.6	1.65-1.92
5.	Glass fiber filled	135-175	70-420	0.2-0.4	1.69-1.95
6.	Macerated Fabric and cord filled	140-190	140-280	0.2-0.9	1.36-1.43
7.	Pulp performed and moulding board	145-175	140-280	0.18-0.8	1.36-1.42
MELAMINE-FORMALDEHYDE MOULDING COMPOUNDS					
1.	No filler	150-165	140-350	1.1-1.2	1.48
2.	Alpha cellulose filled	140-185	105-560	0.5-1.5	1.47-1.52
3.	Cellulose filled	145-180	105-420	0.6-0.8	1.45-1.52
4.	Flock filled	140-165	280-560	0.6-0.7	1.7-2.0
5.	Asbestos Filled	140-170	70-490	0.5-0.7	1.7-2.0
6.	Macerated Fabric Filled	140-165	280-560	0.3-0.4	1.5
7.	Macerated Fabric Filled (Phenolic modified)	150-175	280-560	0.3-0.6	1.5
8.	Glass fiber filled (including nodular)	140-170	140-560	0.1-0.4	1.8-2.0
9.	Melamine Phenol moulding compounds	150-175	140-350	0.4-1.0	1.5-1.7
	UREA Formaldehyde moulding Compound	140-175	140-560	0.6-1.4	1.47-1.52

	Material	Injection Moulding Tempetature ^0C	Injection Moulding Pressure Kg/cm^2	Mould linear shrinkage %mm.mm	Specific gravity
EPOXY RESINS					
1.	Glass Fibre filled	-	-	0.1-0.5	1.6-2.0
2.	Mineral filled	-	-	0.2-0.8	1.6-2.0
3.	Low Density	125-150	70-105	0.6-1.0	0.75-1.00
TYPE - 6					
1.	Unmodified	220-310	-	0.6-1.4	1.12-1.14
2.	Noucleated	220-310	350-1400	-	1.12-1.14
3.	30-35% glass reinforced	-	kg/cm^2	0.4	1.35-1.42
TYPE 6/6					
1.	Coplymer	175-200		0.6-1.5	1.08-1.14
TYPE 6/12			(Limited only		
1.	Unmodified	225-275	by the press	1.1	1.06-1.08
2.	30-35% glass reinforced	225-275	ure required	0.3	1.31-1.38
TYPE 6/10			to fill the		
1.	Unmodified	225-275	mould by	1.2	1.07-1.07
2.	30-35% glass reinforced	225-275	the capacity	0.4	1.31-1.38
TYPE 11			of the		
1.	Unmodified	195-260	machine)	1.2	1.04-1.05
TYPE 12					
1.	Unmodified	180-260	-	0.3-1.5	1.01-1.02
2.	30-35% glass reinforced	228-270	-	0.3	1.23

Material	Compression Moulding Temp.^{0}C	Compression Moulding Pressure Kg/cm^2	Mould linear shrinkage %
DAL Moulding Compounds			
1. Mineral filled	-	-	0.5-0.7
2. Synthetic fibre filled	-	-	0.9-1-1
Epoxy Resins			
1. Glass fibre filled	150-170	-	0.1-0.5
2. Mineral filled	120-170	-	0.2-0.8
3. Low Density	125-150	7-105	0.6-1.0
Polyster			
1. SMC	130-650	21-85	0.05-0.4
2. BMC & TMC	150-190	35-141	0.05-0.4
BMC	150-190	-	0.05-0.6
Silicone Epoxy	180	28-70	0.05-0.6
Cellulosic			
Cellulose Acetate	130-220	565-2260	0.3-1.0
Cellulose Acetate butyrate	130-200	565-2260	0.3-0.9
Cellulose Nitrate	90-370	180	-
Polyimide unifilled	330-370	210-352	-
		210-352	-
40% graphite filled	370	210-352	-
50% Glass fibre reinforced	240	210-706	0.2
Melamine - Formaldehyde Moulding Compounds			
1. No filler	130-165	140-350	1.1-1.2
2. Alpha cellulose filled	140-185	105-560	0.5-1.5
3. Cellulose filled	145-180	105-420	0.6-0.8
4. Flock filled	140-165	280-560	0.6-0.7
5. Asbestos filled	140-170	70-490	0.5-0.7
6. Macerated Fabric filled	140-165	280-560	0.3-0.4
7. Macertated Fibric filled (pheonolic modified)	150-175	140-560	0.3-0.6
8. Glass Fibre filled (including bodular)	140-170	140-350	0.1-0.4
9. Melamine Phenol moulding compounds	150-175	140-280	0.4-1.0

Material	Compression Moulding Temp.^{0}C	Compression Moulding Pressure Kg/cm^2	Mould linear shrinkage %
Phenol formaldehyde and phenol-furfural moulding compounds			
1. No filler	115-160	140-350	1.0-1.2
2. Wood flour and cotton flock filled	145-190	140-350	0.4-0.9
3. Asbestos filled	145-190	140-350	0.2-0.9
4. Mica filled	135-175	70-420	0.2-0.9
5. Glass fibre filled	135-175	140-280	0.0-0.4
6. Macerated fabric and cord filled	140-190	140-280	0.2-0.9
7. Pulp performed and moulding board	145-175	-	0.18-0.8
Compounded with Bustadiene Acrylonitrile copolymers			
8. Wood flour and cotton flock filled	150-180	140-280	0.4-0.9
9. Asbestos filled	155-180	140-280	0.4-0.7
10. Rag filled	155-180	140-280	0.2-0.4
11. Metal filled (iron or lead)	140-160	140-350	0.3-0.4
Urea Formaldehyde molding compound			
Ally to Resins and Monomers	130-160	140-560	0.6-1.4
1. DAP Moulding compound glass filled	150-180	140-420	0.20-0.6
2. DAP Moulding Compound Mineral filled	140-180	170-300	0.10-0.6

MOULD STEELS FOR PLASTICS ABILITY OF STEEL ON HEAT TREATMENT

AISI Type	General Charateristics	Tough ness	Dimensional stability in Heart Treatment	Machineability (Annealed)	Polishability (Heat-Treated)	Typical Applications
P-20	Medium Cartoon (0.30%) and Chrome (1.65%) Available Prehardened (300 Bn) or Annealed (200 Bn)	10	7	9 prehard-ened)	8 prehard-ened)	Excellent Balance of Properties for injection and compression moulds of any size.
H-13	Hot-Work Die Steel;5% chrome, Hardenable to about 50 Rc.	9	8	9	9	Higher Hardness Than P-20';Good Toughness and Polishability, Used for Abrasion Resistance in RP Moulds and High Finish Injection Moulds
A-2	Cold Work Die Steel; High Carbon (1.0%)5% Chrome. Hardenable to About 60 RC	8	9	8	7	High Hardness for Abrasion-Resistant Long-Wearing Compression and injection moulds. Limited to Small Sizes.
D-2	Cold Work Die Steel; Hi Catoon(1.55%) 11.5%chrome. Hardenable to About 60 Rc.	7	9	5	6	Hihest Abrasion Resistance. Difficult to Machine, Susceptible to Strees Cracking Small Moulds Only.
414	Stainless Steel; 12% Chrome, 2% Ni, 1% Hd, Low Carbon (0.03%) Available Prehardened (300 Bn).	10	10	9	9	"Stainless Version" of P-20; Similar Properties and Uses
420	Stainless Steel; 13% Chrome, 0.80% No. Medium Carbon (0.30% Hardenable to About 50 Rc.	9	10	8	10	"Stainless Version" of H-13; Similar Properties and Uses Very Stable in Heat Treatment, Takes High Polish.
4145	Medium Caron (0.50%) and Chrome (0.65%). Available Prehardened	10	10 (Prehardened)	10 (Prehardened)	6 (Prehardened) 7 (fully hard-ened)	Low Cost Steel, for Mold Bases and Large Moulds, Not Suited to High Quality Finish.

DATA ON MOULD SURFACE TREATMENTS

Process	Material	Applied to	Purpose
Coating by impingment molecularly bound	Touhsten'disulfide	Any metal	Redue friction & metal wear with dry film-non - migrating
Coating by impingment organically bound	Graphite[2]	Any metal	Reduce sticking of plastics to mould surface can migrate
Electrolytic plating	Hard Chrome	Steel nickel Copper alloys	Protect polish, reduce wear and corrosion (except for chlorine or florine or florine plastics)
	Gold	Nickel, brass	Corrosion only
	Nickel	Steel and copper alloys	Resist corrossion except sulphur bearing compounds, improves bound under chrome, build up and repair worn or undersized moulds[5].
Electroless	Nickel	Steel	Protect non- moulding surface from rusting
	Phosphor Nickel 4	Steel and Copper	Resist wear and corrosion
Blasting	Fine mesh abrasives (liquid hounding)	Any metal	Remove scale after heat treating. Provide a fine matte finish. Improves release of some theromo-plastics.
	Sand	Any metal	Provide a coarse matte finish
	Steel shot	Steel	Peen, to remove crack and fatigue resistance.
	Glass beads	Any metal	Pen, to remove fine scratches & tool marks
Photo etch	Chemicals	Steel and aluminium	Decorate or "taxture" mould surfaces
Nitriding	Nitrogen gas or amonia	Certain steel alloys	Improves corrosion resistance, reduces wear and galling. Alternate to chrome & nickel plating.
Liquid nitriding	Patented bath3	all ferrous alloys	Improves libricity and minimizes galling.
Anodizing	Electrolytic oxidizing	Aluminium	Hardens surface, improves wear and corrision resistance.

1. Drilube
2. Microseal
3. Tuf-Triding or Lubricasing
4. Kanigen
5. Nicoform

PROPERTIES OF STEEL ON HEAT TREATMENT

			Point Ratings, 1 to 10 (10 being highest)											
Type	AISI Desig-nation	Recom-mended Hardness Rockwell C(b)	Wear Resis-tance	Tough-ness	Compre-ssive Str.	Hot Hard-ness	Corrosion Resis tance	Thermal Conduct	Hobb-ability	Machine ability	Polish-ability	Heat Treat ability	Weld-ability	Ni-tride ability
Pre-Hardened	4130/ 41040 P-20	30-36	2	8	4	3	1	5	1	5	5	10	4	4
Pre Hardened	414SS	30-35	3	9	4	3	7	2	1	4	9	10	4	6
	420SS	30-35	3	9	4	3	6	2	1	4	9	10	4	7
Oil Hardening	01	58-62	8	3	9	5	1	5	5	8	8	7	2	3
	06	58-60	8	4	8	5	1	5	7	10	5	6	2	3
Air Hardening	H-13	46-51	6	7	7	8	3	4	6	9	8	8	5	10
	B7	54-56	7	5	8	8	3	4	6	9	8	8	3	8
	A2	56-60	9	3	9	7	3	4	4	8	7	9	2	8
	A5	56-60	8	4	8	7	2	5	5	10	7	7	4	7
	A10	58-60	9	5	9	7	2	5	5	8	6	7	2	NA
	D2	56-58	10	3	8	8	4	2	4	4	6	9	1	10
Stainless	420SS	50-52	6	6	6	8	2	2	4	7	10	8	6	8
	440 C	56-58	8	3	8	7	2	2	3	6	9	7	4	NA
High Speed	M2	60-52	10	2	10	10	3	3	2	4	6	8	2	10

EFFECT OF ALLOYING ELEMENTS IN STEELS USED FOR MOLD MAKING

Element	Effect
Carbon	Increase strength and brittless; lowers corrosion resistance and conductivity
Manganese	De- Oxidizes, raises strength, ductility, wear resistance
Silicon	De- Oxidizes, raises hardness
Nickel	Austenite stabliser, raises toughness, strength and through - hardness but lowers thermal and electrical conductivity
Chromium	Carbide former; increases hardness, resistance to wear and corrosion; lowers Conductivity
Molybdenum	Increases heat resistance; expands heat treatment range; raises creep strength
Venadium	De- Oxidiser, forms hard carbides; raises fatigue strength
Tungsten	Forms extremly hard carbides, increase hardness and resistance to wear and high temperature; helps to maintain sharp edges (parting lines)
Sulphar	Increase machinability (free machining) but lowers corrosion resistance and weldability and interferes with texturing and plating.

TOOLING MATERIALS RECOMMENDED FOR VARIOUS PLASTICS PROCESSES

Process	TOOLING MATERIAL						
	Plaster	Reinforced Plastics		Wood	Low-Melting Meatals	Cast Aluminium	Stell
		Cast	Liminated				
Thermoforming	x	x	x	x	x	x	
Injection Moulding		x			x	x	x
Compression Moulding		x					x
Foam Molding						x	
Foam Casting	x	x	x	x	x	x	
Plastisol Casting	x	x	x			x	
Reinforcing	x	x	x	x	x	x	

MOULD MATERIALS & ITS APPLICATIONS

S.NO	ISI	Application
1.	T35Cr5M01V30	Cavities, Core, Ejector pins, Guides, Wear Pads of mould
2.	T35Cr5mo1 W1 V30	Die Casting Dies, Plastic Moulds
3.	T35Cr5Mo1 VI	Cavities, Core Ejector pins, Guides, wear pade of moulds
4.	....	High tensile load applications Max. strength when hardened to 58-60 Rc Used for cavity housing core and cavity back plate, shoulder screws, clamps
5.	40Ni2Cr1M028	-do-
6.	13Ni3 Cr80	Cavity and core
7.	....	Bright steels, used for ejector pins, dowels etc.
8.	T105Cr1	Used for guide pillar, Bush and bearing purposes
9.	T103	Used as a wear plate backing pad
10.	....	Delicate core pins in the Mould and Die casting dies
11.	C10 and C14	Bolster, Support, Block, Plates, Backing plate, Holder plate
12.	C35Mn 75	Moulds with a shorter run and on non accurate cavities
13.	40Cr1	Pillar, Bush, Sprue Bush, Locating ring, Bigger Diameter ejector pins
14.	50Cr1 V23	Used for coil and plate springs
15.	T55Ni2Cr65M030	Core, cavity

SPECTRUM OF MATERIALS USED IN BUILDING MOULDS - ARRANGED IN ORDER OF SURFACE HARDNESS AS COMMONLY USED.

Suitable for	Material Class	Suitable for
Thermoplastics Glass filled; Low-Pressure Thermosets SMC BMC; High pressure thermosets; phenolics ureas diallylls melamines alkyds	Carbides Steel, Nitriding Steel, carburizing Steel, water hardening Steel, oil hardening Nickel, Cobalt alloy Steel, prehardened 44 Rc Beryllium, copper Steel prehardened 28 Rc	Thrtmo Plastics Unfilled; Blow Moulds
Prototype Injection Modls : T/P Resins; Structural Foams	Aluminium Bronze Steel low alloy & carbon Kirksite (Zinc alloy) Aluminium, alloy Brass	Vacuum Forming Sheets T/P Resins
Coasting of Liquid Resins	Sprayed metal Epoxy, metal filled Epoxy, not filled Silicone, rubber	

SPECTRUM OF MATERIALS USED IN BUILDING MOULDS - ARRANGED IN ORDER OF SURFACE HARDNESS

Material Class	Surface Hardness		Core Hardness	
Carbides	68-75	Rc	68-75	Rc
Steel, nitriding	>68	Rc	>38	(varies)
Steel, carburizing	60-65	Rc	20-42	Rc
Steel, water hardening	67	Rc	40-55	Rc
Steel, oil hardening	62	Rc	40-60	Rc
Steel, air hardening	60	Rc	60	Rc
Nickel - cobalt alloy	45-52	Rc	45-52	Rc
Steel, prehardened	44	Rc	44	Rc
Beryllium copper	28-42	Rc	28-32	Rc
Steel, prehardened	28-32	Rc	28-32	Rc
Aluminium bronze	188	BHN	188	BHN
Steel, low alloy & carbon	180	BHN	180	BHN
Kirksite (zinc alloy)	80-105	BN①	80-105	BN①
Aluminium alloy	60-95	BN①	60-95	BN①
Brass	50	BN①	50	BN①
Sprayed metal	<50	BN①	<50	BN①
Epoxy, metal filled	85	RM	85	RM
Epoxy, not filled	80-110	RM	80-10	RM
Silicone rubber	15-65	Shore "A"	15-65	Shore"A"

Legend : Rc - Rockwell hardness = "C"scale RM= "M" scale; BHN = Brinell number 3000 kg; BN①= brinell number 500 kg load.

LIST OF MOULD PARTS AND CORRESPONDING STEELS TO BE USED

1.	Back plate (fixed half)	-	Mild Steel
2.	Cavity plate	-	Tool Steel
3.	Core plate	-	Tool Steel
4.	Core backing plate	-	Mild Steel
5.	Riser block or packing blocks or ejector housing	-	Mild Steel
6.	Ejector carrier plate or eject retainer	-	Mild Steel
7.	Eject back plate	-	Mild Steel
8.	Back plate (moving half)	-	Mild Steel
9.	Core	-	Tool Steel
10.	Locating ring	-	Mild Steel
11.	Sprue bush	-	Mild Steel
12.	Locating or guide pin	-	Case hrd & Grd Steel
13.	Locating or guide bush	-	Case hrd & Grd Steel
14.	Sprue snatch and ejector pin	-	Carbon Steel
15.	Ejector pin	-	Carbon Steel
16.	Push back or return pin	-	Carbon Steel
17.	Ejector stop pads	-	Carbon Steel

MOULD FINISH CHARACTERISTICS

	Plating Thickness	Hardness	Co-efficient of Friction	Moulding Temperature	Salt Spary Testint (ASTM)	Finish (SPI)
Chromium	0.00005-0.030 in (0.00127-0.762 mm)	68-70 Rc	0.15	upto 800°F (427°C)	72 hour	A 1
Sulfamate Nickel	in excess of 0.100 in. (2.54 mm)	40-50 Rc	0.22	up to 500 °F (260 °C)	70 hour	A 1
Tungsten Nickel	0.00005-0.002 in (0.00127-0.51 mm)	50-65 Rc	equal to chrome	1200 °F (649 °C)		A 1
Electroless Nickel	0.00005-0.004 in (0.00127-0.10 mm)	49-70 Rc	0.21	up to 700 °F (371 °C)	1000 hour	A 1
Chrome - PTFE	0.0001-0.001 in (0.0025-0.025 mm)	68-70 Rc	0.10	up to 600 °F (316 °C)	500+hour	A 2
Nickel - PTFE	0.00005-0.001 in. (0.00127-0.025mm)	50-68 Rc	0.10	up to 550 °F (288 °C)	1000 hour	A 2
High-phosphorus electroless nickel and hard chrome	0.00005-0.004 in (0.00127-0.10mm)	70 Rc	0.15	up to 700 °F (371 °C)	144 hour	A 1

TYPICAL APPLICATIONS FOR STEELS IN INJECTIONS MOULDS

AISI - SAE Steel designation	General characteristics and uses	Typical heat treatment	
AISI S7 shock -resistant tool steel	Interlocks, latches, sprue bushings	Forging	1120-925^{0}C (finish)
		Normalizing	do not normalize
		Sof annealing	815-845^{0}C
		BHN	197 (max.)
		Strees relieving	675^{0}C
		Carburizing	delivered with Rc 55-58 but may be caburized
		Preheating	590-700^{0}C
		Hardening	925-955^{0}C
		Quenching	air for sections, smaller than 60 mm.oil for sections larger than 60 mm down to 540^{0}C, then air
		Tempering	180 (min.) - 540^{0}C, Rc 50-58
AISI 01 tool steel	Master hobs, plates for gate cutting, small inserts	Annealing	790^{0}C, Rc 62-57
		Hardening	
		Quenching	Oil
		Tempering	
AISI A2 Medium alloy tool steel	Master hobs, slides, plates for gate cutting, cold work	Annealing	900^{0}C
		Hardening	925-980^{0}C
		Quenching air	175-540^{0}C.Rc62-57
		Tempering	
AISI A6 tool steel	Master hobs, plates for gate cutting for cavities requining Optical finish	Anneling	760^{0}C
		Hardening	925-980^{0}C
		Quenching	air
		Tempering	
AISI D2 high carbon, high chromium tool steel	Master hobs,slides,lifters, cold work	Annealing	900^{0}C
		Hardening	980-1025^{0}C
		Quenching	air
		Tempering	205-540^{0}C, Rc 61-54

AISI-SAE Steel designation	General characteristics and uses	Typical heat treatment	
AISI H13 hot work tool steel, Chromium base, generally supplied fully annealed	Cvity plates and iserts, hot hobs, ejector pins, core pins, leader pins, return pins, sprue pullers	Soft annealing Stress relieving Carburizing Preheating Hardening Quenching Tempering Nitriding	850^{0}C Rc9 650^{0}C 900-980^{0}C 600-850^{0}C 980-1080^{0}C air 180 (min.)-500^{0}C,60 Rc 525^{0}C
AISI H23 tool steel	Hot hobs for beryllium- copper hobbing	Annealing Hardening Tempering	880^{0}C 1090-1260^{0}C 650-815^{0}C,Rc 47-30
AISI 1020 tool steel	Ejector plates, ejector retainer plates	Normalizing Annealing Hardening Quenching Tempering	900-955 ^{0}C 540-730^{0}C 870-910^{0}C water or oil 120-205^{0}C
AISI 1030 Carbon steel	Mold bases and structural components such as blocks, spacers, ejector housings,	Normalizing Annealing Hardening Quenching Tempering	870-915^{0}C 675-745^{0}C 855-900^{0}C water or oil optional
AISI 1040 carbon steel	Support pillars	Normlizing Annealing Hardening Quenching Tempering	855-900^{0}C 845-885^{0}C 815-855^{0}C water or oil 315-707^{0}C, Rc 20-26
AISI 1095 carbon steel	Backing plates		
AISI 4130 alloy steel, generally supplied preheat treated	Mold bases and structural components such as cavity retainer plates, support plates, clamping plates	Normalizing Annealing Hardening Quenching Tempering	870 925^{0}C 800-845^{0}C 870-900^{0}C oil 315-705^{0}C, Rc 18-44

AISI-SAE Steel designation	General characteristics and uses	Typical heat treatment	
AISI 4140 alloy steel	Structural components such as retainer plates, support plates, clamping plates	heat treated to approx. Rc 32	
AISI 6150 alloy steel	Sprue bushings	Normalizing	870-900°C
		Annealing	855-900°C
		Hardening	870-900°C
		Quenching	oil
		Tempering	455-565°C, Rc 24-40
AISI 8620 alloy steel	Cast steel	Normalizing	925-955°C
		Annealing	540-650°C
		Hardening	800-830°C
		Quenching	oil
		Tempering	455-565°C, Rc 24-49
AISI S1 tool steel	Master hobs	Annealing	800°C
		Hardening	900-925°C
		Quenching	oil
		Tempering	200-650°C, Rc 58-40
AISI P2 tool steel	Hobbed cavity inserts	Annealing	915°C
		Carburizing	925°C
		Tempering	175-230°,Rc 64-58
AISI P20 tool steel usually supplied prehardened	Machined and hobbed cavity inserts, stripper plates	Forging	1090-925°C (finish)
		Normalizing	850°C
		Soft annealing	700°C, Rc 20
		Strees relieving	550°C
		Carburizing	850-940°C
		Quenching	oil
		Tempering	180(min.-650°C, Rc 28-52
		Nitriding	525°C
AISI 420 tool steel generally supplied fully annealed	Cavity inserts	Soft annealing	780°C
			Rc 18
		Stress relieving	650°C
		Preheating	600-850°C
		Hardening	980-1050°C
		Quenching	air
		Tempering	180 (min.-450°C,Rc 58-66
		Nitriding	not recommended

For more details about the heat treatment of the fore going and other steel grades, it is strongly suggested to consult the corresponding information provided by the steel supplier.

APPLICATIONS FOR THE TYPICAL MOULD STEELS

Type of steel	Typical uses in injection moulds
4130/4140	General mould base plates
P-20	High - grade mould base plates, hot-runner manifolds, large cavities and cores, gibs, slides, interlocks
4414 SS, 420 SS (prehardened	Best grade mould base plates (no plating required), large cores, cavities and inserts
P5, P6	Hobbed cavities
01	Gibs, slides, wear plates
06	Gibs, slides, wear plates, stripper rings
H -13	Cavities, Cores, inserts, ejector pins and sleevs (nitrided)
S 7	Cavities, Cores, inserts, stripperings
A 2	Small inserts in high-wear areas
A6	Cavities, Cores, inserts for high - wear areas
A 10	Excellent for high -wear areas, gibs, interlocks, wedges
D 2	Cavities, cores, runner and gate inserts steel; best polishability
420 SS	Best all - round cavity, core and insert steel; best polishability
440C SS	Small to medium - size cavities, cores, inserts, stripper rings
250,350	Highest toughness for cavities, cores, small unsupported inserts
455M SS	High toughness for cavities, cores, inserts
M 2	Small core pins, ejector pins, ejector blades (up to 5/8 in diam)
ASP 30	Best high - strength steel tall, unsupported cores and core pins

ALLOY STEELS USED IN MOULD MAKING

AISI TYPE	C	Mn	Si	Cr	Mo	Others
1330	0.3	1.75	0.25			
4130	0.3	0.5	0.25	0.9	0.2	
4340	0.4	0.7	0.25	0.8	0.25	2.0 Ni
8630	0.3	0.8	0.25	0.5	0.2	0.7 Ni

STAINLESS MOULD STEELS IDENTIFYING ELEMENTS, IN PERCENT

TYPE	C	Mn	Si	Ni	Cr
T410	0.15	1.00 max	1.00 max.		12.00
T414	0.05	1.00	1.00	2.00	12.00
T420	0.25	1.00	1.00		13.00
T440	0.60/1.20	1.00	1.00		17.50

PRECIPITATION HARDENING STEELS USED IN MOULD MAKING

Universal Nr.	C	Mn.	Si	Cr	Ni	Cu	Others
UNS S15500	0.07	1.00	1.00	15.0	5.0	3.5	0.30 Nb
UNS S17400	0.07	1.00	1.00	17.0	4.5	4.0	0.30 Nb
UNS S17700	0.09	1.00	1.00	17.0	7.00	-	1.01 Al
Properietary	0.2			15.0	4.75	3.2	0.2MO:0.20Cb+Ta

BISMUTH-TIN ALLOYS (CERRO ALLOYS) FOR INJECTION MOULD

Designation (registered trademark)		Cerrptri	Cerrocast
Density	Kg/dm³	8.64	8.16
Melting point or range	^0C	1.38	1.38-170
Specific heat	KJ/Kg	1.88	1.97
Thermal expansion	10^{-6}- K	15	15
Thermal conductivity	W/(K.m)	21	38
brinell hardness BHN	22	22	
Ultimate tensile	strength	MPa	5656
Elongation (slow loading)	%	200	200
X.constant load	MPa	3.5	3.5
Composition			
% Bi	58	40	
% Sn	42	60	

CAST STEELS FOR INJECTION MOULDS; COMPOSITION - TREATMENT - PROPERTIES

Carbon steel	AISI 1020	0.18-0.23% C, 0.30-0.60% Mn, 0.05% S annealed Bh 122, normalized Bh 134 Welding is readly done by most are and gas pricesses. Pre - heating unnecessary unless parts are very heavy
	AISI 1040	0.37 - 0.44% C, 0.60 - 0.90% Mn. 0.04% P.O.05 S normalized and annealed BH 175, normalized and oil quenched BH 225 Welding can be done by arc, resistance and gas processes. To decrease cooling

		rate and subsequently hardness preheating to above 150 preferably 260⁰C. Final heating to 600-650⁰C restores ductility and relieves stress
Alloy steels	AISI 1330	0.28-0.33%C, 1.60 -1.90% Mn. 0.20-0.35% Si, 0.035% P, 0.04%S normalized BH 187, normalized and tempered BH 160 Can be relatively easily welded with mild-steel filler metal
	AISI 4130	0.28-0.33% C, 0.40-0.60% Mn, 0.20-0.35% Si 0.80 - 1.10% Cr, 0.15 -0.25% Mo, 0.35% P, 0.04% S annealed BH175 Welding same as 1330
	AISI 4340	0.38 - 0.33% C, 0.60 -0.80% MN, 0.20-0.35% SI 1.65-2.00% NI, 0.70-0.90% Cr, 0.20-0.30% Mo, 0.035% P, 0.04% S normalized and annealed BH 200 quenched and tempered BH 300 Welding calls for pre-and post heating and filler metals of the same mechanical properties as the base metal. Stress relieving is disirable especially in repair work.
	AISI 8630	0.28-0.30% C, 0.70-0.90% Mn, 0.20-0.35% Si 0.40-0.70% Ni, 0.40-0.60% Cr, 0.15 - 0.25 % Mo normalized Bh 240, annealed BH 175 Welding preferable with filler metal of the same chemical analysis. No preheating needed for sections up to 0.5 in. but strees relieving after welding
Heat - resistant steel	AISI 501	0.10%C, 1.00% Mn, !.00% Si, 4.00% Cr 0.40-0.65% Mo Welding similar to 8530

TECHNICAL DATA OF BERYLLIUM - COPPER ALLOYS

Composition	Be 1.80-2.00% Co/Ni 0.20% min Co/Ni/Fe 0.6% max., Cu balance	Be 1.80-2.00% Co/Ni 0.20% Min Co/Ni/Fe 0.6% max., Pb 0.20-0.6% Cu balance	Be 1.60 -1.79% Co/Ni 0.20% min Co/Ni/Fe 0.6% max., Cu balance	Be 0.20-0.60% Ni 1.40-2.20% Cu balance	Be 0.40-0.75% Co 2.40-2.70% Cu balance
Density Kg/m^3		8250	8415	8610	8775
Thermal conductivity W/(m.K)		130	130	260	260
Thermal expansion 10^{-6}- K^{-1}		17.5	17.5	17.6	18
Electric resistivity $10^{-8}\Omega$.m		7.7	7.7	3.8	3.8
Specific heat capacity J (Kg.K)		420	420	420	420
Moduls of elasticity GPa		131	128	138	138
Tensile strength (MPa)	I II III IV	415-585 620-895 1140-1310 1275	I 415-585 II 620-895 III 1035-1310 IV 1170-1450	I 240-380 II 450-550 III 690-830 IV 760-900	
Yield strength (MPa)	I II III IV	140-415 515-725 1000-1200 1140-1380	I 140-205 II 515-725 III 860-1070 IV 930-1140	I 140-310 II 340-515 III 550-690 IV 690-830	
Elongation [%]	I II III IV	35-60 10-20 3-10 2-5	I 35-60 II 10-20 III 4-10 IV 2-5	I 20-35 II 10-15 III 10-25 IV 10-20	
Rockwell hardness	I II III IV	B45-80 B88-103 C36-41 C35-41	I B45-85 II B91-103 III C32-39 IV B95-102	I B25-50 II B60-75 III B92-100	

Notes: I: Solution heat treated
II: Cold drawn
III: Solution heat treated and age hardened
IV: Cold drawn and age nardened

BLOW MOULD TOOLS MATERIALS

Material	hardness[a]	Tensile Strength (MPa[b])
Aluminum		
No.A356	BHN-80	225
No.6061	BHN-95	275
No.7075	BHN-150	460
Berylium - Copper		
No. 25	HRC-30	930
No. 165	BHN -285	
Steel		
No. 0-1	HRC - 52-60	200
No. A-2	BHN-530-650	
No. P-20	HRC - 32 BHN - 298	1000

#HRC = Rockwell hardness (C scale): BHN = Brinell
"To convert MPa to psi, Multiply by 145

PROPERTIES OF BLOW MOULD MATERIALS

Material	Thermal-conductivity[a]	Wear resistance	Ability to be cast	Ability to be repaired	Density lb/cum (g/cm^3)	Ability to be machined and polished
Aluminum	0.53	poor	fair	good	0.097 (2.699)	excellent
Beryllium-Copper	0.15-0.51	excellent	good	good	0.129-0.316 (3-589-8.793)	fair
Cast iron	0.08	good	good	good	0.24(7.6)	good

a Calories per square centimeter per second per degree centigrade

MARAGING STEELS

Element	C	Ni	CO	Mo	Cr	Ti	AL	Cb
350 Type ,18% Nickel Maraging Steel	0.02	17.50	12.00	4.80	-	1.50	0.10	0.25
300 Type, 18% Nickel Maraging Steel	0.03	18.50	9.00	4.80	-	0.60	-	-
250 Type, 18% Nickel Maraging Steel	0.03	18.25	7.75	4.80	-	0.40	0.10	-
200 Type, 18% Nickel Maraging Steel	0.03	18.25	7.50	4.25	-	0.20	0.10	-
220 Type, 12% Chromium Maraging Stell	0.02	10.00	-	-	12.00	0.35	1.30	-

MOULD MATERIALS - EQUIVALENT STANDARDS

S.No.	ISI	BS	DIN	AISI/SAE	W.nr (Germany)	JIS
01	T35CrMo1V30	BH 11	X38CrMo V51	H 11	-	-
02	T55Cr 5MoW1V30	BH 12	X37CrMoW51	H 12	-	-
03	T35Cr5MoW1	BH 13	-	H 13	-	-
04	-	EN 110	34CrNiMo6	-	-	-
05	40N12Cr1Mo28	EN24	30CrNIMo4	*9840	-	-
***06	13Ni3Cr28	EN 368	14 NiCr14	*3318	-	-
***07	-	BF 1	120WA4	F 1	-	-
(a)08	T10 5Cr1	En31/B13	100Cr	13	-	-
(b)09	T103	BW 18	C10 5W1	W1	-	-
(c)10	C10 & C14	En 2A	-	*1006	-	-
11	C35Mn75	EN8	-	*1040/C1040	-	-
12	40Cr1	EN18	-	*5140	-	-
(d)13	50Cr1V23	EN47	50Cr84	6152	-	-
(d)14	50Cr1V23	En48	-	*5152	-	-
15	T55Ni2Cr65Mo30	-	-	-	-	-
(e)16	-	En 560	X40Cr13	*51420	-	-
17	-	-	-	P 20	-	-
18	-	-	-	H13 improved	1.2344	SKD61
19	- -	-	-	420 Modified	1.2083	SUS420

*	SAE Specification
**	Silver Steel
***	Case Hardening
(a)	Bearing Steel
(b)	Carbon Tool Steel
(c)	Mild Steel
(d)	1% Chromium Spring Steel
(e)	Corrosion resisting, direct quenching steel for moulds used for moulding corrosive plastics.
	Can be used for ther moset moulds, for gate, runners and cavities.

HIGH - GRADE ZINC ALLOYS FOR INJECTION MOLDS

Designation	Density (kg/m^3)	Melting point (^{0}C)	Shrinkage %	Thermal expansion (10^{-6}/ (K)	Tensile strength (MPa)	Elongation (%in 50 mm)	Brinell hardness BH	Compressive strength (MXPa)	Shear strength (MPa)
Zamakl	6700	390	1.1	27	220-240	1-2	100	600-700	300
Kirksite A	6700	380	0.7-1.2	27	226	3	100	420-527	246

GENERAL RECOMMENDATIONS ON STEEL FOR CORE/CAVITY INSERTS

Process		Recommended				
	Theremoplastics Pre-hardened	AISI	DIN	W.nr	JIS	Hardness
Injection.		P2040	CrMnMo7	1.2311	SNCM/30	Rc
	Thermoplastics Thro Hardened	H13X 40	CrMoV51	1.2344	SCM SKD 61	45-54 Rc
	Thermoset	M3:2		1.3344	6062	Rc

Compression/Transfer		H13	X40 CrMnMoV51	1.2344	SKD 61	45-54 Rc
Blow	General	P20	40CrMnMo7	1.2311	SNCM/ SCM	30 Rc
	PVC	420	X42 Cr 13	1.2083	SUS 420	45-50 Rc
Extrusion	General	P20	40 CrMnMo 7	1.2311	SNCM/ SCM	30Rc
	PVC	420	X42 Cr 13	1.2083	SUS 420	45-50 Rc

Note : Chart shows only similar ones not identical equivalents.

AISI : American Iron and Steel Institute
JIS : Japan Industrial Standard
W.nr : Werkstoff (German Standard)
DIN : Deutsches Institut fUr Normung

ALUMINUM ALLOYS FOR INJECTION MOULDS

A.A.No.		7075-T6	1029-T6
Comosition		Al, Zn, Mg, Cu, Cr	Ai, Zn, Mg, Cu
Treatment		Solution treated, artificiality aged	solution treated, artificially aged
Density	kg/dm^3	2.80	2.74
Co-efficient of thermal expansion		23.3X10^{-6}	24.7X10^{-6}
Thermal conductivity	W (kg.m)	140	126
Ultimate tensile strength	MPa	572	537
Yield strength	MPa	503	469
Brinell hardness	BHN	150	125

9

INJECTION MOULD DESIGN

Determination of Number of Cavities based on the machine capacity (Technological method)

Apart, however, from economical considerations, certain other factors have to be taken into account in determining the number of impressions in the mould. So the number of cavities can be determined technologically based on the macine performance.

(i) No. of cavity Based on Shot Capacity (Based on 85% of rated shot capacity

$$Ns = \frac{0.85\ Ms - Rw}{CW}$$

Where

Ns	=	number of cavities based on Shot Capacity
Ms	=	rated Shot Capacity of machine for a particular polymer (gm)
Rw	=	weight of all sprues and runners (gm)
Cw	=	Component weight per cavity (gm)

The volume of moulding is determined by the normal metods of mensuration, while the density of the moulding meterial can be obtained using the information from the meterial manufactures data sheets and the conversion relationships.

(ii) No. of Cavity Based on Plasticising Capacity (Based on 85% of rated Plasticising Capacity)

$$Np = \frac{(0.85\ M\ x Tc) - Rw}{3600\ x\ Cw}$$

Where

Np	=	number of cavities based on machine plasticising Capacity.
Mp	=	rated plasticizing capacity of machine for a particular polymer (gm/hr)
Tc	=	Overall cycle time (sec)

(iii) Determined by Clamping force

$$Nc = \frac{M_c - S_c R_A}{S_c X \; C_A}$$

Where

Nc	=	Number of cavities based on machine clamping force.
Mc	=	rated clamping capacity of machine (Tonnes)
R_A	=	Projected area of all sprues and runners (cm^2)
C_A	=	Projected area of each cavity (cm^2)
Sc	=	design clamping pressure (tf/ (cm^2)

SELECTION OF THE INJECTION MOULDING MACHINE

It is essential to design the mould with the machine requirements and capacity of the machine.

Before mould design is commenced, it is necessary to determine the press capcity that will be required for successful operation, and hence the particular machine to be employed, when the actual machine is known.

The essential considerations are :

1) Short Capacity:
2) Plasticising rate:
3) Clamping force; and
4) Injection Pressure.

(1) SHOT CAPACITY

(a) Plunger Machine

Injection machines are normally rated by the maximum weight of the moulding material that may be injected per shot.

Plunger type of machine is often rated in terms of maximum shot weight with polystyrene. The rating in terms of another material can be determined from the following relation:

$$\text{Shot Capacity With material B} = \text{Shot Capacity With material A} \times \frac{\text{density of B}}{\text{density of A}}$$

Where A is the material used for specification rating of the machine (for example polystyrene) and B is the material actually to used. The above assumes that the bulk factor of the feed material with both polymers is same. If this is not the case of the calculation must be modified by multiplying by the factor

$$\frac{\text{bulk factor of A}}{\text{bulk factor of B}}$$

(b) Screw Machines

The capacities of these machines are normally expressed in cubic centimeters of swept vlume of the injection cylinder. The shot is, therefore, the mass of this volume of plastic melt at the plasticizing temperature and pressure. Thus

Shot Capacity (gm) = Swept Volume (cm^3) x Density of melt at plasticising temperature and pressure (gm/cm^2)

Altermatively, ignoring the effect of pressure, it may be estimated from

Shot Capacity (gm) = Swept Volume (Cm^3) x d x c

Where d = Density of plastic at normal temperature in gm/cm^3
and c = correction for percent volume expansion of the plastic at the moulding temperature.

Approximately for Crystalline materials c = 0.85
while for amorphous materials c = 0.93

An empirical factor can alternatively be used to give a more conservating shot capacity on Screw injection machines, providing an allowance for leakage of screw head non return valves and so on.

Shot Capacity in (gm) = Swept volume of cylinder (in cm^3) x F

Where F = 0.5 for polystyrene and ABS
0.4 for polystylene
0.38 for polystylene

The machine selected, therefore, must be capable of injection sufficient material at each shot to meet the estimated weight of the moulding including the runner and sprue . This would comprise the weight of all mouldings in the case of multi - impression moulds.

2. Plasticising Rate

The plasticising rate is expressed as the number of Kg of material that the machine can bring per hour to moulding temperature.

Polysterene is often the standard material on which the plasticising rate is base, but the actual value will depend upon the particular material to be moulded.

The plasticising rate is a function of the heating capacity of the machine, hence the amount of material that can be brought to moulding condition in a given time is dependent upon the moulding temperature necessary and the specific heat of the material.

The plasticising rate of a machine with any material B can be determined approximately from the machine specification plasticising rate based on material A (often polystyrene) from the formula.

$$\text{Plasticising rate of material B (gm/hr)} = \text{Plasticising rate of material A (gm/hr)} \times \frac{Q_A\text{(Cal/gm)}}{Q_b\text{(Cal/gm)}}$$

Where Q is the total thermal capacity of the material at moulding temperature (i.e.,) (Specific heat x temperature rise) + latent heat of fusion. Values of Q may be obtained from Table.

Empirical Values

The plasticizing capacity of the machine, where standard rating is based on polystyrene is
60% for moulding polypropylene or low density polyethylene and
50% for moulding high density polyethylene

Rough plasticising rates, making allowance for the slow screw speeds required for some materials and intermittent use of the screw between injection cycles, can be determined form the factor.

$$\frac{\text{recommended screw speed for material}}{\text{maximum screw speed possible on machine}} \times \frac{\text{Continuous output at maximum screw speed}}{2}$$

3. CLAMPING FORCE

The clamping force (Tonnes) available in the machine controls the maximum projected area of the moulding that can be produced. The injection pressure of the plastic material within the mould develops a force which tends to open the mould. This force is proportion to the projected area of the moulding and feed systems and must be opposed by the available machine clamping force.

Because of the various losses occuring in the heating cylinder, nozzle and feed systmes only a proportion of the pressure produced by the cylinder is transmitted to the cavity.

$$\text{Clamping force required (Kgf)} = \text{Projected area of moulding (cm}^2\text{)} \times \text{1/3 to 1/2 times the injection pressure (Kgf/cm}^2\text{)}$$

The projected area means including runners . For multiple impressions, the area of all cavities must be included.

Lower clamping values can be used with screw type of machines owing to the lower injection pressure possible with these machines. Typical design values are as follows :

	Clamp Pressure (Tonnes/cm²of projected area)	
Type of Machines	Easy flow grades	Other grades or high flow path/cavity thickness rations
Plunger	3	5
Screw	1.5	2-3

A more detailed guide to clamping pressure requirements for screw injection moulding of polyolefins and polystyrene based on flow path length.

4. INJECTION PRESSURE

The injection pressure may be found from the following :

$$\text{Injection pressure (Kgf/cm}^2\text{)} = \text{Injection hydraulic line gauge pressure} \times \frac{di^2}{dp^2}$$

Where

di = diameter of injection cylinder (cm) and
dp = diameter of heating cylinder ram (cm)

On many plunger injection machines, $\frac{di^2}{dp^2} = 20$

The injection pressure required for moulding a component may very depends on type of plastic materials. The injection pressure must be regulated in order to produce satisfactory parts economically. Pressure needed to mould a particualr article depends on

- the flow characteristics of the moulding materials;
- the thickness of the moulding section;
- the cavity depth;
- the projected area of the piece part;
- flow length and
- type, size and finishing of the feed systems.

This section require high injection pressure to fill and thus need more clamping force to prevent the mould opening due to higher force developed inside the cavity. The injection pressure of a particular machine can be obtained from the machine manufacture's data sheet or it can be calculated.

THE DISIGN OF RUNNER :

There are some consideration for the designer to keep in mind during designing of runner for a particular mould :

- the shape and cross section of the runner
- the size of the runner and
- the runner layout

1. Shape of the Cross Section of the Runner

The various crossections of the runner is shown in fig. The cross section should be as small as possible. But still compatible with plastics flow requirements. This can be achieved in some instances by special shapes.

A circular cross section provides the largest flow area for the least mass but is more expensive to produce becase the runner must be cut into two plates. Hence machining is more expensive.

A trapeziodal cross section is best because it is easier to machine. Being tangential to a circle the flow is as good as in circular cross section; however, the mass of plastics is 30% greater.

A flat runner has reduced flow but will cool faster than either a circular or trapeziodal runner. Finally, runner shaped as crosses provide better cooling because of their larger surface. They also provide stiffening to the runner during ejection, but are more expensive to manufacture; they are rarely used.

The runner efficiency is depends upon the cross sectional area and the periphery of the runner.

$$\text{Runner Efficiency} = \frac{\text{Cross section area}}{\text{Periphery of the Runner}}$$

The various cross section and the efficiency of the runners for comparative purpose is given in fig.

Choice of Runner

For simple two-plate moulds which have a flat parting surface the fully round runner or hexagonal runner is to be preferred, the increased mould cost is relatively small. For moulds which have complex parting surfaces, where it would be difficult to match accurately, the semicircular channels of the round runner or, for multiplate moulds, the trapezoidal or modified trapezoid should be useds.

2. Runner size

When deciding the size of the runner the designer must consider the following factors :

- The wall section and volume of the moulding;
- The distance of the impression from the main runner or sprue;
- Runner cooling consideration;
- The range of mould maker's cutter available and

- The plastics material to be used.

The following empherical formula is used to find the size of the runner or branch runner for moulding upto 200 gm. and with sections less than 3 mm. For rigid PVCs and acyrilics, the increase the calculated diameter by 25%

$$D = \frac{\sqrt{W} \times \sqrt[4]{L}}{3.7}$$

Where

D = runner diameter (mm)
W = weight of moulding (gm)
L = length of runner (mm)

(i) The runner should not be below 2 mm diameter, nor above 10 mm or 13 mm diameter where ever applicable.

(ii) The calculated size should be increased to the next suitable cutter size.

Theritically the cross- sectional area of the main runner should be equal to the area of the branch runners. But this relationship is, however, ignored when the maximum diameter is reached,

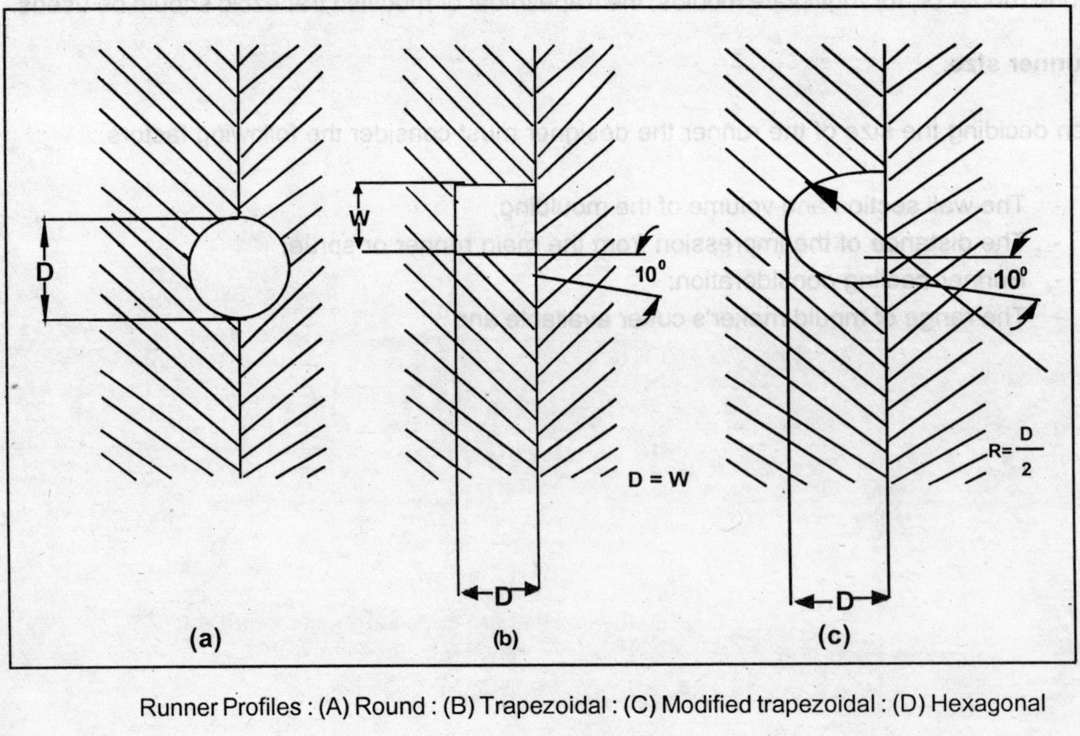

Runner Profiles : (A) Round : (B) Trapezoidal : (C) Modified trapezoidal : (D) Hexagonal

Runner profiles : (a) round; (b) trapezoidal; (c) modified trapezoidal; (d) hexagonal

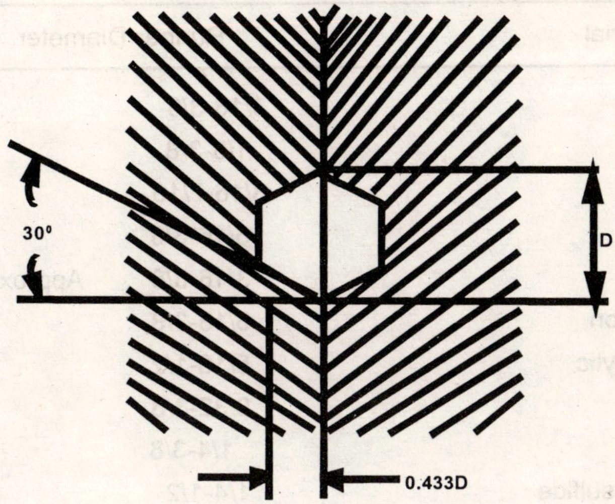

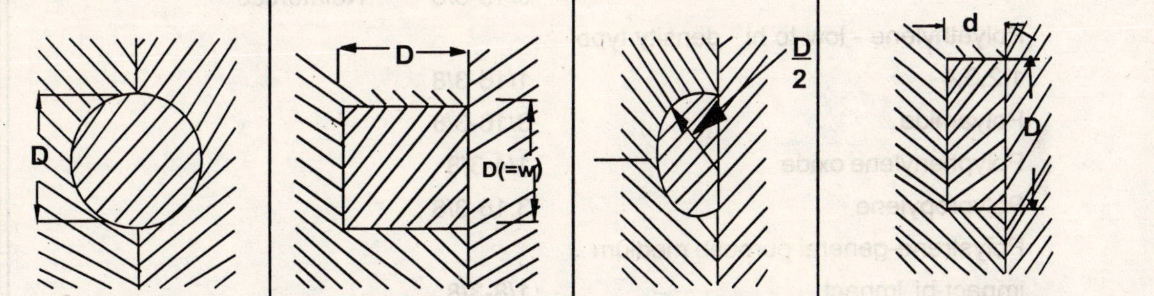

ROUND	SQUARE	SEMICIRCULAR	RECTANGULAR
0.25 D	0.25 D	0.153 D	d = $\frac{D}{2}$ 0.166D $\frac{D}{4}$ 0.1D $\frac{D}{6}$ 0.071D

$$\frac{\text{AREA}}{\text{PERIPHERY}} \text{ RATIO}$$

Efficiency of various runner profiles (the higher the value the greater the efficiency

The Table gives an idea abot the runner size for various unfilled themoplastics materials.

RUNNER DIAMETERS FOR UNFILLED MATERIALS

Material	Runner Diameter	
ABS, SAN	3/16-3/8	
Acetal	1/8-3/8	
Acetate	3/16-7/16	
Acrylic	5/16-3/8	
Butyrate	3/16-3/8	Approximate
Fluorocarbon	3/16-3/8	
Impact acrylic	5/16-1/2	
Ionomers	3/32-3/8	
Phenylene	1/4-3/8	
Phenylene sulfide	1/4-1/2	
Polyallomer	3/16-3/8	
Polycarbonate	3/16-3/8	
Polyester thermoplastic	1/8-5/16	Unreinforced
	3/16-3/8	Reinforced
Polyethylene - low to hi - density type 1,2,3,4	1/16-3/8	
Polyamide	3/16-3/8	
Polyphenylene oxide	1/4-3/8	
Polypropylene	3.16-3/8	
Polystrene-general purpose medium impact-hi impact	1/8-3/8	
Polysulfone	1/4-3/8	
Polyvinyl chloride (plasticized)	1/8-3/8	
PVC Rigid (modified)	1/4-5/8	
Polyurethane	1/4-5/16	

the weights of runner systems in grammes for material density 1 gm/cm^3

Runner diameter (mm)	Weight (g) per cm length of runner	
	Round	Trapezoidal
2	0.0314	0.0366
3	0.0707	0.0823
4	0.1256	0.1463
5	0.1963	0.2286
6	0.2826	0.3292
12	1.1304	1.3167
15	1.7663	2.0574
18	2.5434	2.9626

For other materials multiply the above value by the relative density.

PRESSURE DROP IN RUNNER SYSTEM

The quantity of viscous fluid flowing through the round and rectangular channells given by

$$Q = \frac{\pi d^4 \Delta p}{2^7 \mu L} \quad \text{(for round runner).........(1)}$$

$$Q = \frac{W t^3 \Delta p}{2^5 \mu L} \quad \text{(for rectangular runners).......(2)}$$

d = diameter of runner;

Δp = pressure drop in runner system;

μ = coefficient of viscosity;

L = Length of runner or gate;

W = width of runner;

t = depth of runner or gate;

q = quantity of material flowing through the runner per second.

Equation (1) and (2) may be written as

$$\Delta p = \frac{K1L}{d^4} \quad ......(1)$$

$$\Delta p = \frac{K2L}{t^3} \quad ..... (2)$$

Where K1 and K2 and are constants for a particualr for a particular runner and material under fixed condition.

With plastics material, the coefficient of viscosity is dependent upon the temperature and in any injection proces this will change because of the heat losses taking place with in the runner system. This loss will be a direct function fo the length of the runner and the speed of the injection. The heat losses will also tend to change the effective channel diameter 'd' as the frozen skin adjacent to the surface of the runner become at location remote from the sprue.

For simplicity the changes in viscosity may be taken as a function of runner length and the pressure loss in the runner system as a function directly proportional to the 1.25th power of the runner length. Thus

$$\Delta p = K1L^{1.25} \quad \text{or} \quad \Delta p = K2L^{1.25} \quad ......(3)$$

Assuming that the inner diameter or dimensions are constant throughout the system, then

$$K1 = \frac{2^7 Q \mu}{\pi d^4} \quad \text{and } K2 = \frac{2^5 Q \mu}{wt^3}$$

It is also seen from these equation that the quantity of material flowing is directly proportional to the fourth power of the runner diameter, thus any small increase in the diameter results in a substantial increase in ease of flow.

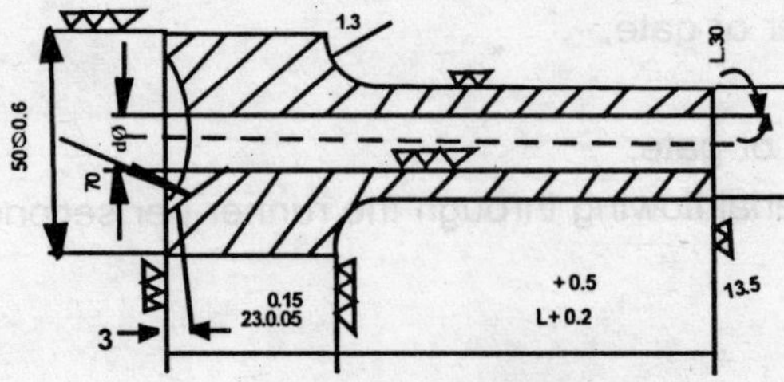

SPRUE BUSH

SPRUE SIZES FOR POLYSTYRENE

Weight of the moulded part (g)	Minimum sprue diameter (mm)
10	3.5
10-20	4.5
20-40	5.5
40-150	6.5
150-300	7.5

For other materials the sprue diameter should be multipled by the following factors:

Acrylic	-	2.0
Softend	-	0.8
Nylon	-	0.8
Cellulose acetate	-	1.0
Ployethylene	-	0.5

2. Rectangular edge gate

The dimensions of the gate are given by width (W), depth (h) and land length (L) L=0.75 mm (To reduce pressure drop, this should be kept minimum)

Sometimes L is equal to the gate diameter or depth.

The cross sectional area of the gate = h x W

h = n.t

Where

t = wall section thickness

n = material constant

The values of 'n' varies with different types plastic materials.

Material	Value of 'n
Group 1. Polystyrene, Polythylene	0.6
Group 2. Polyacetal, Polycarbonate, Polypropylene	0.7
Group 3. Cellulose acetate, Polymethyl / methacrylate, Nylon	0.8
Group 4. P.V.V.	

$$W = \frac{n\sqrt{A}}{30}$$

where A = Surface area of cavity (mm^2)

Overlap gate

The gate may be used for all common moulding materials apart from rigid PVC. The size of the gate can follow the general pattern applied for the rectangular gate with the same limitations.

L1 = 0.5 - 0.75mm (distance between the end of the runner and the wall of the impression)

Gate width $W = \frac{n\sqrt{A}}{30}$

Gate height h = n.t

Gate length = L2 = $h + \frac{W}{2}$

Fan Gate

This type of gate may be used with all moulding materials except certain grades of P.VC. Because of the larger width of the impression this type of gate is more suitable for large area thin all moulding. Since a large volume of material can be injected in a short time.

Land length L = 1.3mm

width $W = \frac{n\sqrt{A}}{30}$

height h 1 = n.t

depth of gate at the runner = h2 = Wh1/D

The width W increase normally from the basic runner diameter. But the depth 'h"decrease for the purpose to have a constant cross-sectional area throughout the length of the gate.

The effective length of the gate land between the runner and the impression progressively increase from a minimum at the centre line to a maximum at the outer gate.

Tab gate

Tab gates were designed specifically for use with acrylic material in order to obtain strees free high optical clarity mouldings. The restriction between the runner and tab causes the material to impinge at high velocity on the side of the tab, which breaks the jet and the materials is highly turbulated prior to entry into the moulding cavity.

tab width (Y) = D (diameter of the runner)
tab depth (X) = 0.9 (t = wall thickness of the moulding)
tab length (Z) = 105 D Minimum

Diaphragm gate

The diaphragm is useful for producing, for instance, busings, with the highest possible degree of concentricity while avoiding weld lines. The necessity of having to remove the gate by means of subsequent machining is a disadvantage, as is the support of the core on only one side.

a. Gates are made 0.38 mm to 0.76 mm thick

b. The land length (L) should be a minium consistant with the strength of the steel left between the circular runner and the impression.

L = 0.75 mm to 1 mm is preferred.

c. h1 = 0.7 n.t
L1 - n.t

The depth of diaphragm gate is normally made less than the values recommended for the rectangular gate.

Disc or Ring gate

This is used preferably for internal gating of cylindrical parts in order to eliminate disturbing weld lines. With fibrous reinforcements such as glass fibres. for instance. the disc gate can reduce the tendency for distortion. in this case must not have a plain bottom otherwise air trapping and burning of material will take place.

The gate is in the form of concentric film between the runner and impression. The dimensions are identical with the diaphragam gate.

L = 0.75 - 1 mm
h = 0.7 n.t

Flash (or) Film gate

This type of gates is mainly used to obtain flat moulded parts with few moulded - in stresses and warpage free products. A film gate over the entire width of the moulded part is useful in providing a uniform flow front. A certain tendency of the melt to advance faster in the vicinity of the sprue can be offset by correcting the cross section of the gate. In single cavity moulds, however, the eccentric location of the gate can lead to opening of the mould one side, with subsequent formation of flash. The film gate is usually trimmed off the part after ejection, but this generally does not impair automatic operation.

The film gate is similar in principle to the diaphragm gates in that it provides for a large flow area and results in quick fill time.

The gate depth	h =	0.7 n.t
land length	L =	1.3 mm (min)

Pin Point Gate

This type is particularly desirable for use with materials which give differential shrinkage characteristics and it often used as an alternative to film gating. This type of gate is often used for mult-point feeding and for single off-centre feeding.

To prevent gate fracturing the area of moulding adjacent to the gate, particularly with the more brittle materials, it is desirable to taper the gate. so that the gate is caused to break at the junction with the secondary sprue.

Land length L = 0.75 to 1 mm suitable

gate diemeter d = n.c. $\sqrt[4]{A}$

Where A = surface area of the cavity (mm)

C = function of the wall section thickness (t)

Gate balancing on Multi-Impression Moulds

Where cavities are of different shot weights, the gate size of one cavity may be established arbitrarily and the remainder sized by applying one of the formulae below.

For round gates

$$d_2 = d_1 \left(\frac{W^2}{W^1} \right)^{1/4}$$

While for rectangular gates (assuming gate width constant)

$$t_1 = t_1 \left(\frac{W^2}{W^1} \right)^{1/3}$$

Where d_1 = the gate diemeter of the first cavity (cm.)

d_2 = the gate diameter of the second cavity (cm.)

t_1 = depth of gate in first cavity (cm.)

t_2 = depth of gate in second cavity (cm.)

W_1 = Weight of first cavity component (gm.)

W_1 = Weight of second cavity component (gm.)

STRENGTH OF CAVITY

a. Wall thickness in Rectangular Cavities

The maximum deflection commonly allowed in such moulds is 0.13 - 0.25 mm depending upon the size of the mould. Of this, 0.1 - 0.2 mm may be due to clearances between the blocks of the built - up mould and elongation of the bolster or register faces. For strees design purposes, therefore, a maximum deflaction of 0.025-0.05 mm is usually taken. the approximate thickness of the side wall required may be calculated from the following formula.

$$y = \frac{C_p \ d^4}{Et^3}$$

$$\text{or } t = \sqrt[3]{\frac{C_P \ d^4}{E\,y}}$$

where Y = deflection of side walls (cm)

C = constant (See Table below)

P = maximum cavity pressure (kgf/cm^2)

d = total depth of cavity wall (cm.)

E = modulus of elasticity for steel (2.1 X 10^6 kg f/cm^2)

t = thickness of cavity wall (cm)

Ratio of the length of cavity wall Of the depth of cavity wall	Value of C
1 : 1	0.044
2 : 1	0.111
3 : 1	0.134
4 : 1	0.140
5 : 1	0.142

b. Cylindrical Cavities

Increase in radius due to the internal pressure of the injected material can be determined from

$$r^1 = \frac{rp}{E}\left[(R^2 + r^2)\,(R^2 - r^2) + m \right]$$

where	r1	=	increase of inside radius (cm.)
	r	=	original inside radius
	R	=	original outside radius (cm.)
	m	=	Poisson's ratio (0.25 for steel)

DETERMINATION OF SUPORT PILLAR REQUIREMENTS, STREES CALCULATION

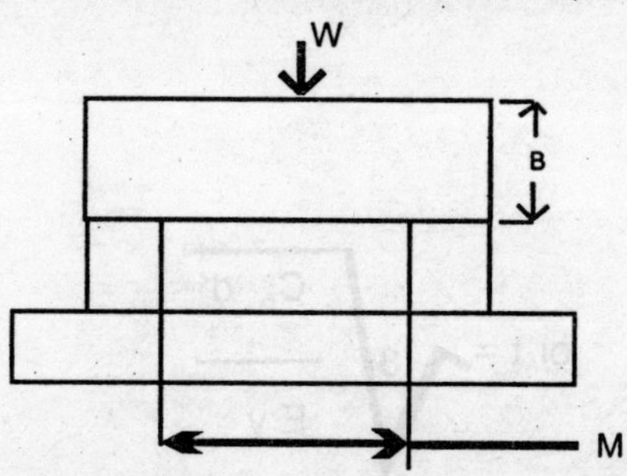

$$W = \frac{8\ ZS}{M}; \qquad Z = \frac{LB^2}{6}; \qquad A = \frac{W}{P}$$

W = Permissible load on support plate (kgs)

S = Permissible working strees (kg/Cm^2) 840 kg/cm^2

M = Distance between supports (cm)

L = Length of support plate (cm)

Z = Section moduls (cm^3)

B = Thickness of support plate (cm)

P = Max. unit pressure on support plate (kg/ (cm^2)

= 630 kgs/cm^2

A = Permissible projected area of moulding/impression (cm^2)

If the calculated permissible projected area (A) is found less than actual projected area of moulding than it denotes that additional support pillars are required to with stand the stresses.

STRENGTH OF GUIDE PILLARS

The guide pillar sysem is primarily concerned with alignment of the mould faces as they close during the moulding cycle. But in certain cases the pillars have also the subsidiary functions of protecting the core and acting as locating pins when the mould is being assembled.

The side of the guide pillars is of great important in the mould. The working diameter of the pillars and the number of guide pillars will depend on the size of the mould and whether or not a side force is likely to be exerted on it. So the guide pillars should withstand side forces to be exerted on it. The moulds with deep and heavy cross - sectional cores exert side thrusts and the guide pillars should be strong enough to absorb them without any damage.

The side force acting on the guide pillar can be calculated from equation.

$R = 2/3\ p_f(d_c h_c)$ (kgf) for circular cores

where

d_c = Max. dia of core (cm)

h_c = Height of core (cm)

p_f = cavity pressure causing side thrust taking into consideration the effect of clamping force (kg/cm^2) say 300 kg/cm^2

$R = a_c\ h_c\ p_f$ (kgf) for rectangular core.

where

a_c = max. side of core (cm)

h_c = height of core (cm)

p_f = say 300 kgf/cm^2

then the working diameter of the pillar can be determined based on the side thrust acting on it Cross sectional area of the pillar = $\frac{\pi d^2}{4}$ (cm)

where d = working diameter of the piller (cm)

The strength of guide pillar = area x shear strees of the steel material.

For steel, shear strees (fs) = 1600 kgf/cm²

N = No. of guide pillars in a mould.

$$\# R \leq \frac{\pi d^2}{4} fs. N$$

$$d^2 \geq \frac{4R}{N\, fs. \pi}$$

$$d\ (cm) \geq \sqrt{\frac{4R}{N\, fs. \pi}}$$

The surface of the pillar must be hard and wear-resisting. This is achieved by machining the pillar from a low carbon steel which is then case hardened. this process gives a surface which resists pick-up and scoring as the pillar continuosly enters and leaves the bush.

If the guide pillar is likely to be subjected to bending forces the use of a carburising nickel chrome steel to be preferred. The normal size range of guide pillars obtainable as standard parts (to reduce mould cost these should be used wherever possible) in between 10 mm and 38mm working diameter; Some very large moulds may require guide pillars outside this range.

The range of sizes of pillar adopted.

Size of mould (mm x mm)	Working diameter of the pillar (mm)
100 X 100	10
100 X 150	13
150 X 200	16
200 X 250	19
250 X 300	22
300 X 400	25
400 X 600	32
600 X 700	38

Tolerance Grade :

Mould plate bore and fitting diameter of the pillar-H7/n6
Guide bush bore and working diameter of the pillar - H7g6

THERMAL PROPERTIES OF PLASTICS

Material	heat distortion temp^{0}C	Specific heat	Bulk factor	Total heat cal/g	Thermal diffusivity cm 2. Sec-1/ ^{0}C 10^{-3}
ABS	98	0.35	1-8-2.0	72	1.7
Acetal (homopolymer)	-	0.35	-	105	0.7
Acetal (copolymer)	140	0.35	1.8-2.0	111	0.72
Acrylic	85	0.35	1.8-2.0	72	1.09
Nylon 66	180	0.40	2.0-2.1	135	1.01
Nylon 610	-	0.40	-	116	0.90
Nylon 11	-	0.58	-	153	0.95
Nylon 6	160	0.38	-	125	0.98
Nylon 66 GF	230	0.30	-	103	1.33
Polycarbonate	140	0.30	1.73	84	1.47
Polyethylene LD	-	-	1.84-2.3	-	-
MFI 2	60	0.55	-	193	1.17
MFI 7	-	0.55	-	182	1.15
MFI 20	90	0.55	-	160	1.09
Polyethylene HD	90	0.55	1.725-1.9	171	1.57
Polyephenylene oxide	-	0.32	1.3-2.2	93	1.53
Polypropylene	120	0.46	1-9-1.96	130	0.65
Polystyrene	90	0.32	1.9-2.15	57	0.6
PVC (rigid)	60	0.24	2.3	38	1.16
PVC (flexible)	70	0.40	2.2	56	0.7
Cellulose Acetate	70	0.36	2.4	63	1.04
SAN	90	0.33	1.9-2.15	66	0.81
CAE	70	0.35	2.2	63	1.27

Thermal Conductivity of Plastics and Metals Details (Cal/Sec. cm^{0}C)

	x 10^{-4}		x 10^{-4}
ABS (acrylonitrile Butadiene Styrene)	6	Polystyrene	2.0
Acetal (homo and copolymer)	5.5	Polyvinyl chloride rigid	4.0
Acrylic	4.5	flexible	3.4
Nylon 66	6.0	Cellulose acetate	4.8
Nylon 610	5.3	CAB	4.7
Nylon 11	8.8		
Nylon 66 glass filled	7.0	Copper	1.043
Polycarbonate	5.3	Brass	0.204
Polyethylene LD	8	Steel	0.115
Polythylene HD	11.5	Aluminium	0.502
Polyphenylene oxide	5.2	Zinc	0.264
Polypropylene	3.3	Wood	0.0006

RECOMMENDED FITS USED IN INJECTION AND COMPRESSION MOULD

S.No.	Description	Type of fit	Injection	Compression
1.	Main guide pillar - main guide bush	Slack running fit		H7/e7
2.	Main guide pillar - main guide bush	Close running fit		H7/g6
3.	Main guide pillar & Bush housing	Light keying fit	H7/k6	H7/k6
4.	Sprue bush - Cavity insert or housing	Medium drive fit	H7/m6	
5.	Core pin - cavity insert	Slide fit	H7/h6	H7/h6
6.	Side moving core or sliding block - guide slot	Close running fit	H7/g6	H7/g6
7.	Cavity Insert housing	Light keying fit	H7/k6	H7/k6
8.	Finger cam housing	Light keying fit	H7/k6	H7/k6
9.	Push back pin - cavity insert or cavity nest	Close running fit	H7/g6	H7/g6
10.	Ejector pin - cavity insert	Close running fit	H7/g6	H7/g6
11.	Cavity insert	Slide fit	H7/h6	H7/h6

12.	Alignment bush - Housing	Close running fit	H7/ g6	H7/g6
13.	Ejector guide pin - Housing	Medium drive fit	H7/ m6	H7/m6
14.	Ejector guide pin - Ejector guide bush	Close running fit	H7/g6	-
15.	Ejector guide pin - Ejector guide bush	Slak running fit	-	H7/e7
16.	Ejector guide bush - Ejector retainer	Light Keying fit	H7/k6	H7/k6
17.	Ejector guide bush - Ejector plate	Running fit	H7/f7	H7/f7
18.	Rest button - Housing	Heavy drive fit	H7/m6	H7/m6
19.	Register ring - M/c platen	Running fit	H7/f7	-
20.	Register ring - Housing	Running fit	H7/f7	-

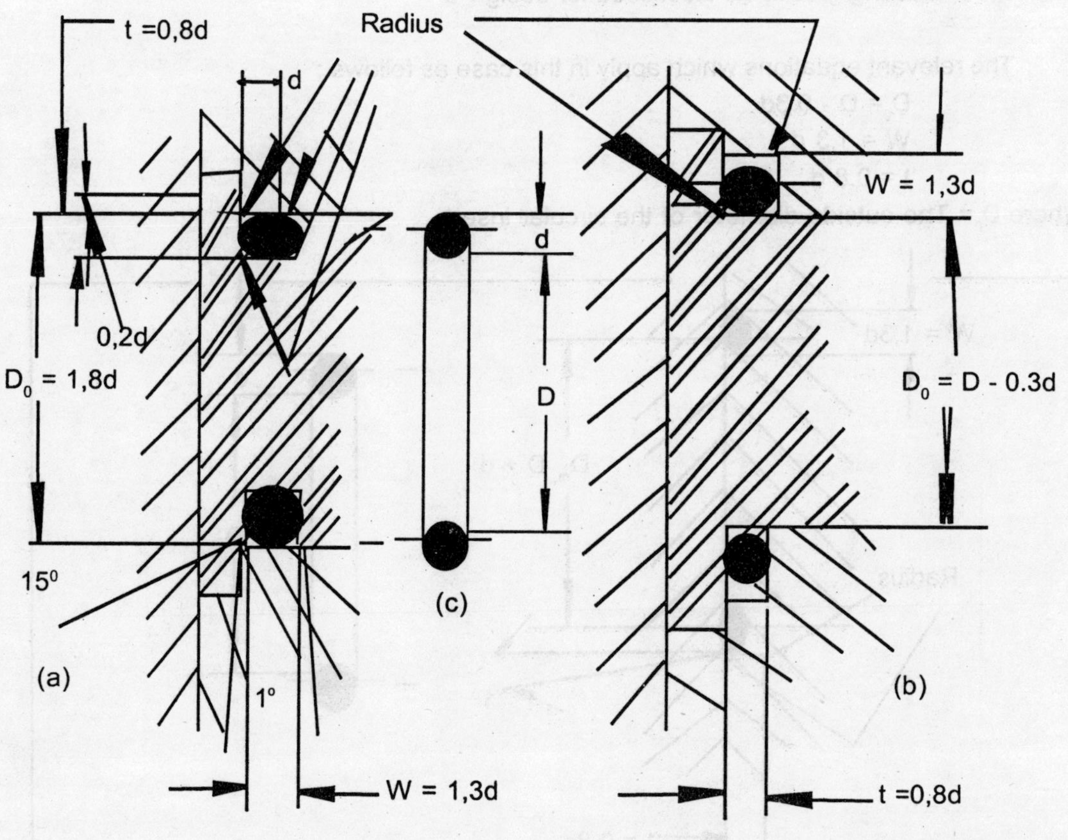

O- ring fitting details for sealing a curved surface

Useful equations which may be used a guide to the dimensions of the recess in this case are as follows :

D_0 = 1.8 D
W = 1.3 d
t = 0.8 d

Where D_0= the outside diameter of the circular insert.
All other symbose are designated above.

In this design the lowe O - ring is accommodated in a recess machined into the mould plate adjacent to the fitting diameter of the insert. Note that this design necessitates a larger than normal flange. The advantage of this design is that it eliminates the necessity of stretching the O - ring in order to fit it into its
accomodating groove as discussed for design 'a'

The relevant equations which apply in this case as follows :

D_0= D - 0.3d
W = 1.3 d
t = 0.8 d

Where D_0= The outside diameter of the circular insert.

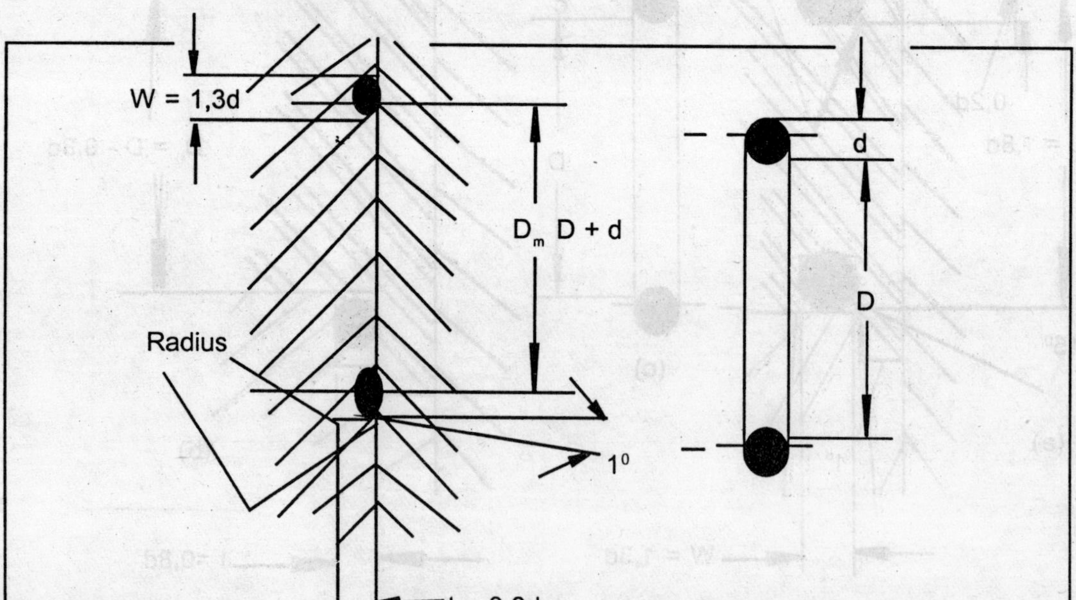

O-ring fitting details for sealing a flat surface

O- ring fitting details for sealing a flat surface

Useful equations which may be used as guide to the dimensions of the recess are as follows :

$D_m = D + d$

$W = 1.3\ d$

$t = 0.8\ d$

Where D = the inside diameter of the O - ring

D_m = the mean diameter of the O - ring

d = the cross sectional diameter of the O - ring

W = the width of the recess at its base.

t = the depth of the recess.

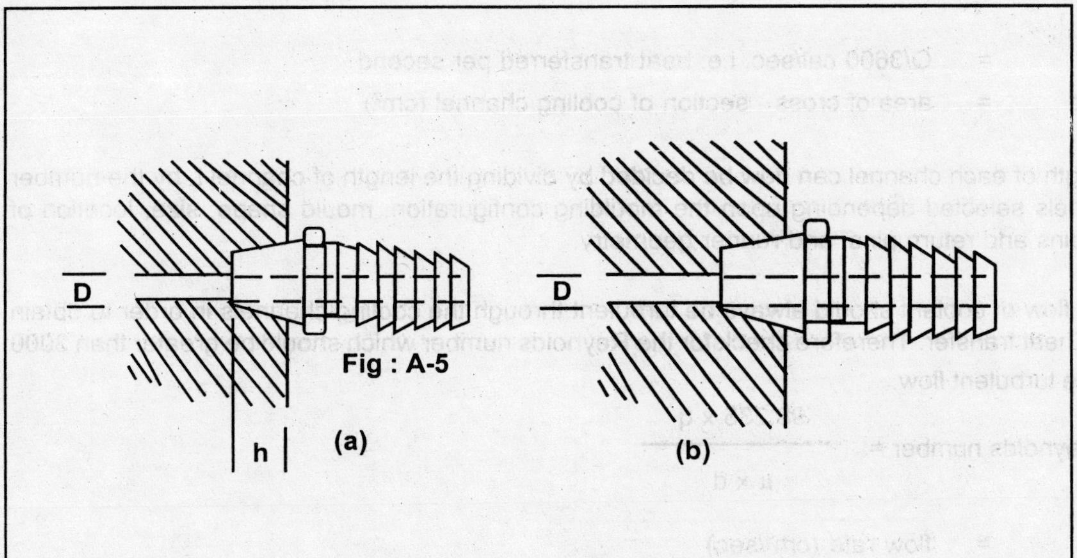

Fig : A-5

Adaptor (BSP)	Tapping drill Size (in)	Depth of threaded hole (mm)	(in)	Diameter of flow - way: Method A (mm)	(in)	Method B (mm)	(in)
1/8	11/32	11	7/16	8	11/32	-	-
1/4	29/64	13	1/2	11	7/16	7	1/4
3/8	19/32	13	1/2	15	19/32	10	3/8
1/2	47/64	14	9/16	18	23/32	13	1/2

Adapts for coupling mould water circuit to supply

TOTAL LENGTH OF THE CHANNEL

$$L\ (CM) = \frac{Q1\ .Z}{YS\ \{_{mat} \ -- \ T\ _{mould}\} - 2\ A_c}$$

Where

Q_1 = Q/3600 cal/sec. i.e. heat transferred per second

Ac = area of cross - section of cooling channel (cm^2)

Length of each channel can now be decided by dividing the length of channel L by the number of channels selected depending upon the moulding configuration, mould shape, size, location of ejector pins and return pins, and runner geometry.

The flow of coolant should always be turbulent through the cooling channels in order to obtain the best heat transfer. Therefore check for the Reynolds number which should be greater than 3000 to ensure turbulent flow.

$$\text{Reynolds number} = \frac{98.235 \times q}{\mu \times d}$$

q = flow rate (cm^3/sec)

μ = viscosity of the liquid in centistokes (water = 1)

d = diameter of the cooling channel (cm)

MOULD COOLING

Heat to be extracted from tool per hour

This is expressed by Q_c measured in cal. Then

$$Qc = m [C_p (T_1 - T_2) + L]$$

Where m = weight of plastics material injected per hour into tool (g)

Cp = specific heat capacity of polymer (cal/g deg C)

T_1 = injection temperature (^{0}C)

T_2 = tool temperature (^{0}C)

and L = specific latent heat of fusion of polymer (cal/g)

Alternatively, if total heat per unit mass of plasticised material is known, then

$$Q^c = m \times a$$

where a = total heat content of plasticised polymer (cal/g)

and m = weight of material as before.

Amount of cooling water required per hour to dissipate the heat is derived from

$$Q = km_2 (T_3 - T_4)$$

where m_2 = weight of water passed through tool (g/hr)

T_3 = outlet temperature of water (^{0}C)

T_4 = inlet temperature of water ($^0C^0$)

Q = rate of extraction of heat (cal/hr)

K = constant to allow for heat transfer efficiency.

Some sample values of this constant are for

Cooling channels bored in cavity plate or male cores K = 0.64

Cooling channels bored in back plates K = 0.5

Cooling channels using embedded copper pipes K = 0.1

For effective cooling

$$Q_c = Q$$

so that

$$m_2 = \frac{m[C_p(T_1 - T_2) + L]}{K(T_3 - T_4)} \quad \text{or} \quad m_2 = \frac{m \times a}{K(T_3 - T_4)}$$

COOLING TIME

The minimum cooling time for a moulding may be estimated from a formula derived by Ballman and Shusman. This has been shown to give good results with polystyrene, but is also useful as an approximate guide for other materials.

$$S = \frac{-t^2}{2\pi} \log_e \frac{(T_x - T_m)}{4\,(T_c - T_m)}$$

where S = minimum cooling time (s)

t = thickness of moulding (cm)

= thermal diffusivity of material (cm^2/s)

T_x = ejection temperature of moulding (often heat distortion temperature is used (^0C)

T_m = mould temperature (^0C)

T_c = cylinder temperature (^0C)

EJECTION SYSTEM

All the therm plastic materials contracts as they solidify, which means that the moulding will shrink on to the core which forms it. This shrinkage makes the moulding difficult to remove. Ejection should be possible in action and ejectror pin also placed in a position that the ejection marks will not be seen on the product when it is in normal use. it is advisable, if possible, to use a type of ejection mechanism, which does not have any marks on the moulded product. Incorrect placing of ejector pin can cause distortion on the moulded product by exerting pressure in the wrong place. Ejector pins and blades should always be made from a hardened steel to avoid undue wear which will cause flashing on the moulded part. well planned and well constructed ejector mechanism contributes considerably to the efficiency working and life of a mould.

TYPES OF EJECTION :

There are different types of ejection are in use and a particular system has to be selected depends upon the configuration of the product. The designer must selected the type of the ejection and the location of the ejector pins carefully so that there should not be any witness marks visible on the product when it is in use. The different types of ejector systems which are generally used in moulds are as follows.

Although there is no proven method of determining in advance. The number of ejector pins required, a rough rule of thumb is to provide 1 cm^2 area of ejector pin bearing surface for every 100 cm^2 of side wall contact.

Pin Ejection

This is the most common type of ejection as, in general, it is the simplest to incorporate in a mould. The working diameter of the ejector pin must be a good slide fit in its mating hole in the mould plates. If it is not, then plastics material will creep through the clearance. Once the size of the ejector pins has been decided upon, the greater will be the effective ejection force and the less the likelihood of distortion occuring.

FORCE REQUIRED IN EJECTION

All thermoplastic materials contact as they solidify, which means that the moulding will shrink on to the core which forms it. This shrinkage makes the moulding difficult to remove. So that force required to strip the component or moulding will depends on several factors such as.

- the area of contact between moulding and mould faces in line of draw.
- co - efficient of friction between the plastic and steel materials,
- elastic modulus of the steel material,
- thickness of the moulding,
- poisson's ratio of the plastic material, and
- thermal contraction of plastic material.

So the force required to strip a moulding from a male core may approximately be determined from

$$F = \frac{S.\ E.\ A.\ \mu}{d\left(\dfrac{d}{2t} - \dfrac{d}{4t}\gamma\right)}$$

where

F = ejection force required (kgf)
S = thermal contraction plastic across diameter, 'd'

	=	(co - efficient of thermal expansion) x (them. difference between soltening point and ejection temp.) x d (cm)
t	=	thickness of moulding (cm)
A	=	total area of cotact between moulding and mould faces in line of draw (cm^2)
E	=	elastic modulus (Kgf/cm^2)
μ	=	Co-efficient of friction plastic and steel
d	=	diameter of circle of circumference equal to length of perimeter of moulding surrounding male core (cm)
ϒ	=	poisson's ratio of the plastic/across diameter d (0.4 to 0.5 on an aver age)

Type of plastics	Co - efficient of friction of Plastics with steel	Thermal expansion $/^0C \times 10^{-5}$	Softening point ^0C
ABS	0.5	6 - 13	85
Acetal	0.25	8.1	175
Acrylic	0.4	5 - 9	90
Nylon	0.4	8 - 13	Melt point 200 - 220
Polycarbonate	0.55	7.00	165
Polyethylene (LD)	0.4	16 - 18	86
Polyethylene (HD)	0.25	11 - 13	125
Polypropylene	0.33	11	150
Poly styrene	0.4	6 - 8	90
Polystyrene (toughened)	0.5	3.4 - 21	88
PVC	0.55	5	82
SAN	0.5	6.5	94

10

COMPRESSION & TRANSFER MOULD - POT CALCULATIONS

The clamping pressure provided by the chamber is an important consideration. If the total cavity area is greater than the total pot area, the hydraulic pressure exerted by the plastic compound would tend to open the mould at the parting line. to ensure perfect mould locking, the area (AP) should be 25% - 30% greater than the combined area of the moulding surface and the area of all runners and sprue/s.

The dimensions of the pot, if it is round or square can be calculated once the area is known.

Total area of pot A_p = Total project area of cavities, runners and sprue + 25 - 30% of total projected area.

Volume of pot Vp = Total volume of all the piece parts, the runners and the sprue plus approximate valume of a small amount for a 0.5 to 1 mm thick cull multiplied by Bulk factor of the com pound.

$$\text{Depth of pot} = \frac{V_p}{A_p}$$

CALCULATION ASPECTS

1. Ram Load

(a)

Transfer ram load required (tonf or tf) = area of transfer plunger (in^2 or cm^2) x pressure required to transfer moulding material ($tonf/in^2$ or tf/cm^2)

The pressure required for transfer moulding the particular material to be employed may be obtained from the material manufacture's data, e.g. for phenolic 3-6 $tonf/in^2$ (472-945 kgf/cm^2)

(b) Main ram load required to clamp mould (tonf or tf) = pressure developed by transfer ram ($tonf/in^2$ or tf/cm^2) X

$$\times \left[\text{Projected area of moulding at flash face, including runners (in}^2\text{- or cm}^2\text{)} + \text{(bottom transfer) area of transfer pot (in}^2\text{ or cm}^2\text{)} \right]$$

A safety margin of clamp over transfer moulds pressure of 10-20% is added

(C) To maintain balance where transfer moulds employ and intergral pot;

$$\text{Area of pot (in}^2\text{ or cm}^2\text{)} = \text{Projected area of mould cavities and runners (in}^2\text{or cm}^2\text{)}$$

With adequate gates and runners the projected area of the mould may sometimes exceed that the pot, although conservative practice adopts the reverse-the area of the pot exceeding that of the mould by amounts varying Iron 10 to 25%

Press tonnage required for integral for integral pot moulds is given by

$$\text{Main ram load (tonf or tf)} = \text{area of transfer pot plunger (in}^2\text{ or com}^2\text{)} \times \text{pressure available to transfer moulding material tonf/in}^2\text{ or lf /cm}^2\text{)}$$

2. Electrical Energy Requirements to Heat Mould

Empirical - 20-40 W/kg of mould.

By calculation

The heat required to raise the mould to operating temperature is given by

$$Q_R=Q_1+Q_2+Q_3+Q_4$$

While the heat required to maintain the mould at operating temperature and to provide heat for curing plastic material is given by

$$Q_o=Q_1+Q_2+Q_3+Q_5$$

Where Q1 = Conduction losses through asbestos insulation from mould to platens (Btu/h or cal/h)--(a)

Q2 = radiation losses from mould faces (Btu/h or cal/h)--(b)

Q3 = convection losses from mould facess (Btu/h or Cal/h)--(c)

Q4 = heat required to raise temperature of metal to operating remperature (Btu or Cal)--(d)

Q5 = heat required for heating plastic material (Btu/h or cal/h)--(e)

(a) $Q1 = \dfrac{KA_1\, \Delta T_1}{L}$

where K = thermal conductivity of asbestos insulation (fps or cgs units)

A_1 = total area of mould top and bottom faces in contact insulation (ft2 or cm2)

L = total thickness or top and bottom asbestos insulation (ft^2 or cm^2)

ΔT_1 = temperature difference between mould and press (deg C)

(b) $$Q_2 = 1.38 \times 10^{-9}(T_2 + 460)^4 \times A_2$$

where $1.38 \times 10^{-9}(T_2 + 460)^4$ is the modified Stefan's constant for a rough finished tool surface

T_2 = temperature of mould (deg F or deg C)

A2 = area of exposed tool faces (ft^2 or cm^2)

During intial heating up, the tool is normally closed an hence normally the only radiation losses are from the vertical faces, In operation, however, the horizontal faces are exposed for a proportion of the time and hence an additional allowance must be made when determining the heat requirements during moulding.

(C) The heat lost by convection from the vertical faces is

$$Q_3 = \left(0.7 + \frac{\Delta T_3}{375}\right) \Delta T_3 A_2$$

where ΔT_3 = temperature difference between tool and surrounding air (deg F or deg C).

During initial heating up the tool is normally closed and hence the only convection losses in normal cases are from the vertical faces considered above in operation, however, the horizontal faces are exposed when the tool is open so that losses from these faces must be taken into account when determining the heat requirements during moulding.

The heat lost by convection from faces vertical lying upwards is

$$Q_3 = \left(0.7 + \frac{\Delta T_3}{375}\right) \Delta T_3 \times 1.1 \times A_3$$

The heat lost by convection form horizontal faces lying downwards is

$$Q_3'' = \left(0.7 + \frac{\Delta T_3}{375}\right)\frac{\Delta T_3}{2} A_4$$

where A_3 = area of mould face lying upwards (ft^2 or cm^2)

and A^4 = area of mould face lying downwards (ft^2or cm^2).

(d) The initial heat required to raise the tool from room temperature to operating temperature, additional to the heat losses listed, is

$$Q_4 = m_1 \times Cp_1 \times \Delta t_4$$

where m_1 = weight of mould (lb or kg)

C_{p1} = specific heat capacity of mould steel

ΔT_4 = temparature rise from room temparature to operating temparature (deg F or deg C).

(e) Heat required to cure the moulding material is given by

$$Q_5 = m_2 \times Cp_2 \times \Delta T_5$$

where m_1 = weight of moulding material (lb/h or kg/h)

C_2 = specific heat capacity of moulding material

ΔT_5 = temparature rise required from room (or pre-heat temparature) to moulding temperature (dog F or deg C).

Example

K	=	thermal conducitivity of asbestos	=	0.21 Btu/ft2/h/degF/ft
A_1	=	area of top and bottom mould faces	=	2.0 ft^2
T_2	=	temparature of mould	=	350 deg F
ΔT_1	=	temparature difference between mould and press	=	350 deg F
L	=	combined thickness of asbestos insulation	=	0.1 ft
A_2	=	total exposed area of vertical tools faces	=	3 ft^2
A_3	=	area of mould face lying upwards	=	1 ft^2
A_4	=	area of mould face lying downwards	=	1 ft^2
ΔT_3	=	temperature difference between tool and surrounding air	=	290 deg F
m_1	=	weight of tool	=	300lb
C_{p1}	=	specific heat capacity of mould steel	=	0.11 Btu/lb deg F

ΔT_4	= temperature rise from temperature to operating temperature	=	290 deg F
m_2	= weight of moulding material	=	9 lb
Cp_2	= specific heat capacity of moulding material	=	0.4 Btu/lb deg F
ΔT_5	= temperature rise from room temperature to moulding tempeature	=	290 ded F

(i) Heat required to raise mould to operating temperature

$$Q_R = Q_1 + Q_2 + Q_3 + Q_4$$

where

$$Q_1 = \frac{0.21 \text{x} 2.0 \text{x} 200}{0.1} \text{ Btu/h} = 840 \text{ Btu/h}$$

$$Q_2 = 1.38 \text{x} 10\text{-}9\ (350+460)^4 \text{ x } 3 \text{ Btu/h} = 1{,}782 \text{ Btu/h}$$

$$Q_3 = \left(0.7 + \frac{290}{375}\right) 290 \text{ x } 3 \text{ Btu/h} = 1{,}281 \text{ Btu/h}$$

$$Q_4 = 300 \text{ x } 0.11 \text{ x } 290 \text{ Btu} = 9{,}570 \text{ Btu}$$

Therefore, heat required to bring mould to operate temperature in four hours is given by

$$Q_R = 4\ (840 + 1{,}782 + 1{,}281) + 9{,}570$$

= 24,582 Btu 25,182 Btu

= 24,582 Btu/h 25,182 Btu

$$= \frac{24{,}582}{4} \text{ Btu/h} \qquad \frac{25{,}182}{4} \text{ Btu}$$

= 6145 Btu/h 6295 Btu/h

Since heat losses will be lower during the earlier stages of heating up, the operating temperature will be reached in practice somewhat earlier than calculated,

(ii) Heat required to run the tool during moulding, assuming that the mould remains open during one half of cycle

$$Q_0 = Q_1 + Q_2 + Q_3 + Q_5$$

where Q1 = 840 Btu/h

$$Q2 = 1.38 \text{ x } 10^{-9}\ (350 + 460)^4 \text{ x } \left[A_2 + \left(\frac{A_2 + A_4}{2} \right) \right] \text{ Btu/h}$$

$$= 1.38 \times 10_{-9}\,(350 + 460)^4 \times \left[\, 3 + \left(\frac{1+1}{2}\right) \right] \text{ Btu/h}$$

$$= 2376 \text{ Btu/h}$$

$$Q_3 + Q'_3 + Q''_3 = \left(0.7 + \frac{290}{375}\right) 290 \times \left[\, A_2 + (1.1A_3) + \frac{1}{2}\left(\frac{A_4}{2}\right) \right] \text{ Btu/h}$$

$$= \left(0.7 + \frac{290}{350}\right) 290 \times [3 + ½\,(1.1 \times 1) + ½\,(½)] \text{ Btu/h}$$

$$= 1{,}624 \text{ Btu/h}$$

$$Q_5 = 9 \times 0.4 \times 290 \text{ Btu/h}$$

$$= 1{,}044 \text{ Btu/h}$$

= Therefore the heat required to maintain mould heat during moulding

$$Q_0 = 840 + 2{,}376 + 1{,}624 + 1{,}044 \text{ Btu/h}$$

$$= 5{,}844 \text{ Btu/h}$$

Electrical heating

1 kWh = 3,412 Btu

1 Btu = 0.29 Wh

SELECTION MOLDING METHOD- COMPRESSION OR TRANSFER

Factors to Consider: **Advantages-Limitations**	**Compression**	**Transfer**
Close tolerances, projected area		●
Close tolerances, over flash line, minimum flash		●
Lowest mold shrinkage	●	
Uniform shrinkage, all directions	●	
Maximum uniform density	●	
Reduced cure, thick sections		●
No weld lines, less molded-in strains	●	
Small holes, longer length, through holes	●	
Extremely thin mold sections, telescoping		●

No venting promblems	●	
Impact strength	●	
Molds with movable sections or cores		●
Large prjected area parts	●	
Lowest mold-flash scrap	●	
Generally less mold maintenance		●
Gate or sprue removal necessary		●
Maximum number cavities per clamp force	●	
Mold erosion, sprues, runners, gates		●
Generally higher mold cose		●

ECONOMIC DETERMINATION OF THE NUMBER OF CAVITIES IN MOULDS

n	-	the total number of parts to processed
x	-	number of mould cavities
t (minute)	-	period of pressing + change of piece using a mould with x cavities
G (Rs)	-	Production and maintenance cost of a cavity
A1 (Rs)	-	Production cost of the mould using
r	-	workshop overheads calculated with the wages in decimal fractions
a (Rs/hr)	-	wage per hour of a worker
K = a (1+r) (Rs/hr)	-	the hourly wage plus operating costs
P(Rs)	-	total manufacturing cost of the n pieces to be produced (including mould production costs)

It is evident that

$$P = \frac{n}{x} . t . \frac{K}{60} + G + A1$$

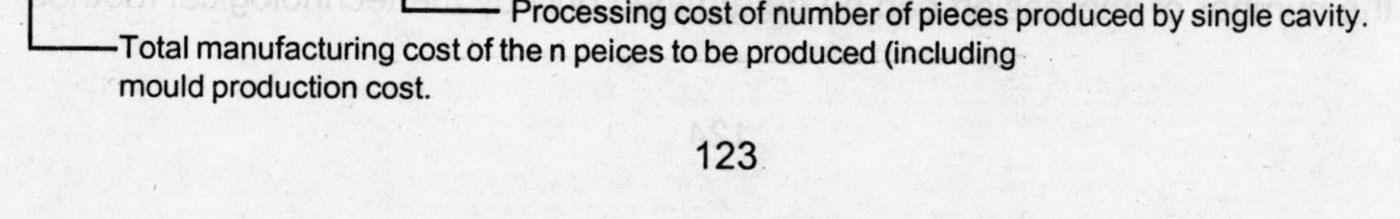

This cost, as a function of the number of cavities has a minimum value when,

$$\frac{dp}{dx} = 0$$

$$\frac{dp}{dx} = \frac{dp}{d}\left(\frac{nt\,k}{60}\,x\text{-}1 + G + A1\right) = 0$$

where n, t, k, G, and A_1 are constants for a particular case.

$$\therefore \quad \frac{dp}{dx} = \frac{ntk}{60}\,(-1)\,x^{-2} + 0 + A_1 = 0$$

$$\frac{dp}{dx} = \frac{-ntk}{60x^2} + A_1 = 0$$

$$\therefore \; -\frac{ntk}{60\,x^2} + A1 + 0$$

$$A_1 = \frac{ntk}{60\,x^2}$$

$$\therefore \quad X^2 = \frac{ntk}{60\,A_1}$$

The most economical number of cavities is

$$X = \sqrt{\frac{ntk}{60\,A_1}} \quad \text{--------(2)}$$

It should be noted that the results of the formula (2) could be considered as an aproximate value and the economical number of cavities should be checked technologically. For example there may not be enogh clamping power available in the machine, therefore a mould with a limited number of cavities is used.

This method of calculating the number of impression is practically impossible during design stage. So the number of impression can be determined only by the technological method.

11

BLOW MOULD DESIGN ASPECTS

BLOW MOULDING TEMPERATURES AND PRESSURES

Polymer	Melt Temp- (⁰C)	Blow Mould Temp. (⁰C)	Blowing Pressure (Pa x 10)⁵
Acetal	193-216	93-149	6.9-10.0
Acrylic	205-232	93-104	5.5
ABS	199-204	93-104	2.7-6.9
Polyester (PET)	270-300	2-54	5.5-6.9
Polyethylene	260-282	82-93	6.9
Polyethylene			
LDPE	140-160	4-21	3.4
HDPE	170-190	4.21	5.5
LLDPE	170-199	4-21	5.5
Polypropylene	190-220	4-21	5.2-6.9
Polystyrene	185-230	66-93	2.7 - 6.9 (1)
PVC	150-180	10-21	5.2-6.9

TOLERANCE GUIDELNES FOR BLOW MOLDED PARTS

Division of Nominal Dimensions		
Above	Below (inclusive)	Tolerance
-	3	± 0.3
3	6	± 0.4
6	10	± 0.5
10	18	± 0.6
18	30	± 0.8
30	50	± 1.0
50	80	± 1.2
80	120	± 1.4
120	180	± 1.6
180	250	± 2.0
250	315	± 2.5
315	400	± 3.0
400	500	± 3.5
500	630	± 4.5
630	800	± 5.6
800	1000	± 7.0

Wall Thickness

For cost competitiveness, plastic parts are designed with the minimum wall thickness required for part strength and performance. In addition, each plastic material has a range of thickness in which it is most easily processed.

WALL THICKNESS GUIDELINES FOR COMMON MATERIALS*

Material	Minimum in. (mm)	Maximum in. (mm)
ABS	0.030 (0.76)	0.125 (3.18)
Acetal	0.015 (0.38)	0.125 (3.18)
Acrylic	0.025 (0.64)	0.250 (6.35)
Nylon (amorphous)	0.030 (0.76)	0.125 (3.18)
Nylon (cryltalline)	0.015 (0.38)	0.125 (3.18)
Phenolic	0.045 (1.14)	1.000 (25.4)
Polycarbonate	0.040 (1.02)	0.400 (10.2)
Polyester (T/P)	0.025 (0.64)	0.125 (3.18)
Polyester (T/S)	0.040 (1.02)	0.500 (12.7)
Polyethylene (HD)	0.020 (0.51)	0.250 (6.35)
Polyethylene (LD)	0.030 (0.76)	0.250 (6.35)
Polypropylene	0.025 (0.64)	0.300 (7.62)
PPO (modified)	0.030 (0.76)	0.400 (10.2)
Polystyrene	0.030 (0.76)	0.250 (6.35)
PVC	0.040 (1.02)	0.400 (10.2)

These values are for rigid and semirigid materials. Formed and flexible materials vary from these values.

PROPERTIES OF BLOW MOLD MATERIALS

Materials	wear Resistance	Ability to be Cast	Ability to be Repaired	Density Lbs./Cum.	Ability to be Machined and Polished
Aluminium	Poor	Fair	Good	0.097	Excellent
Beryllium Cooper	Excellent	Good	Good	0.129-0.316	Fair
Cast Iron	Good	Good	Good	0.24	Good

RECOMMENDED BLOW MOULD TOOL MATERILS AND THEIR PROPERTIES

	Hardness rockwell "C" Brinell	Tensile strength (Psi)	(MPa)	Thermal conductivity (Btu/in/ft²h⁰F)	(W/M⁰K)
Aluminium					
A356	BHN-80	36.975	255	1.047	151
6061	BHN-95	39,875	275	1.165	168
7075	BHN-150	66,700	460	905	130
Beryllium copper					
25	RC-30	134,850	930	728	105
and	(BHN-285				
Steel					
0-1		0-1			
and	Rc-52-60	290,000	2,000	243	35
A-2	(BHN-530-650)				
P-20	RC-32	145,000	1,000	257	37
	(BHN-298)				

RECOMMENDED MOULD SHRINKAGE VALUE FOR DIFFERENT PLASTIC MATERIALS

Materials	Longitudinal shrinkage (in/in or mm/mm)
Acetal	0.025-0.035
Celiulose acetate	0.003-0.007
Nylon	0.01-0.02
Phenoxy	0.003-0.004
Polyethylene	0.005-0.01
Polyethylene Low density	0.015-0.03
high density	0.03-0.04
Polypropylene	0.02-0.035
Polystyrene	0.002-0.008
toughened	0.003-0.01
Polyvinyl choloride	0.003-0.01
Styrene acrylonitrile	0.003-0.004

These values are typical of part shrinkage for materials used in blow molding . Shrinkage numbers will vary with different grades of the same material manufactured by a different process. Operating conditions such as cooling time and temperature will greatly influence the amount of shrinkage that occurs after the part is molded.

Shrinkage (%)	Shrinkage %	
	Polyethylene	PVC
Longitudinal shrinkage	2.1± 0.1	0.36± 0.04
Transverse shrinkage	1.9± 0.2	0.13± 0.05
Neck length shrinkage	3.7± 0.1	0.98± 0.16

SUGGESTED PINCH-OFF DESIGN PARAMETERS

Container Volume, V (liters)	Pocket Opening Angle,∞	Welding Edge Width, b (mm)	Pocket Width, C	Compression Bar Width L	Gap Between Compression Bars, X	Delayed Closing Travel, W (mm)	Delayed Closing Speed (mm/s)		
							HDPE		PP
							HDPE	MMW	
≤1	30°	0.6-1	2d	2b-3b	0.1c	2d-4d	40-80	140-260	75-100
1-30	30°	1-3	2d	2b-3b	0.1c	2d-4d	10-40	75-140	20-75
30-250	30°	3-5	1d-1.5d	2b-3b	0.1c	2d-4d	3-10	10-75	10-20
250-200	30°	5-7	1d-1.5d	2b-3b	0.1c	2d-4d	3-10	-	-

OTHER PARAMETERS RELATED TO BLOW MOULD DESIGN

Head- Die Design

Bottle weight

Where no significant parsion draw -down occurs (i.e) excluding large/long parisons extruded very slowly) the relationship between bottle weight and die/mandrel dimensions may be determined approximately from the formula

$$W = C\pi D_m \; tLS^2$$

where W = weight of moulding including neck flash (g)

L = length of moulding or parision including pinch - off flash (cm)

D_m = mean diameter of die annuals (cm)

t = annulus gap (cm)

S = die swell ratio for polymer concerned

C = constant for polymer concerned

= 0.78 (metric units)

This formula applies directory to landed (fixed gap) dies only. On machines with parison control (variable die gap), appropriate modifications have to be made to calculation in accordance with the parison thickness profile adopted.

EFECT OF SHEAR RATE ON DIE SWEEL OF VARIOUS THERMOPLASTICS

	Die swell ratio at 200°C			
	Shear rate (s - 10)			
	10	100	400	700
Acrylic, high impact	1.17	1.27	1.35	1.42
Polyethylene low density	1.45	1.58	-	-
high density	1.49	1.92	2.15	2.35
Polypropylene copolymer	1.52	1.84	2.1	-
Polypropylene homopolymer	1.61	1.9	2.05	-
Polystyrene	1.37	1.7	1.88	-
toughened	1.22	1.4	-	-
Polyvinyl chloride, high impact	1.35	1.5	1.52	1.53

Parison Daiameter Calculation

Pinch - off length should not exceed 80% of base width. Parison diameter may be determined from the following formula, but not exceed two-thirds width of the container.

$$Dm = \frac{D}{S}$$

$$= \frac{2L}{\pi S}$$

Where D = parison dimameter (cm)

L = pinch - off length (cm)

Parison sag. $\left(\frac{L}{V_0 T} - 1\right)$ may be determined

$$p \frac{gL^2}{6\mu V_0} = \tan^2 \sqrt{\frac{pgv_0\ t^2}{6\mu}}$$

Where l = parison length

g = acceleration due to gravity

μ = melt viscosity

V_0 = extrusion rate

p = melt density

t = parison extrusion time.

Blow - up ratio

The blow - up or bottle/parison diameter ratio normally should be below 3:1 but can be increased for special design requirements.

Die land length Determination

The following ratios apply :

Die aperture	Land Length
<0.03 in (0.76 mm)	<1 in (25.4 mm)
0.03-0.1 in (0.76-2,5 mm)	1 in (25.4 mm)
> 0.1 in (2.5 mm)	> 1 in (25.4 mm)

Alternatively a working relationship can be used of
Die land = 8 x die annulus width.

Clearance between pich - off plates below pinch off itself (pinch - off clearance) = 1.8 x parison wall thickness

Large blow mouldings % 5 gals or 20 ltr) require a dam behind the pinch- off prevent thining of pinch off.

Mold Shrinkage

Material	Shrinkage, Inches/inch* Contimeters/centimeter) of dimension
HDPE	0.020
PP	0.018
TPE	0.016
HDPE, 25% mica filled	0.016
ABS	0.005- 0.008
PC	0.005- 0.007
PVC (rigid)	0.003- 0.006
PS	0.005- 0.007
Nylon, 15% glass	0.003- 0.005

These values are typical of part shrinkage for materials used in blow molding. shrinkage numbers will vary with different grades of the same material manufactured by a different process. Operating conditions such as cooling time and temperature will greatly influence the amound of shrinkage that occurs ofter the part is molded.

*Inch values given; centimeter values are proportionally equivalent.

Typical Blow Molder Size and Capacity

Typical sizes of equipment for the various extrusion blow - molding processes. Very large parts can be produced by accumulator head machines, while high - volume , smaller parts can be produced by the other processes.

Part weight, lb (kg)	Extruder Output lb/h (kg/h)	Number of Heads	Platen Size. in (cm)	Clamp Pressure ton (kN)
		Continuous Extrusion		
Under 1	100-500 (45 - 227)	1-4	24 x 24 (61 x 61)	20 (179)
1 - 5	300-1300 (136 - 590)	1-4	30 x 24 (76 x 61)	33 (295)
		Continuous Extrusion		
Under 1	200 (91)	1-2	18 x 24 (46 x 61)	20 (179)
5	500 (227)	1-2	30 x 40 (76 x 102)	40 (358)
15	900 (408)	1-2	42 x 48 (107 x 122)	100(896)
35	1300 (590)	1-2	50 x 60 (127 x 152)	150 (1344)
300	1850 (839)	1-2	60 x 80 (152 x 203)	200 (1792)
		Reciprocating Screw		
Under 1	300 (136)	1-2	15 x 24 (38 x 61)	40 (358)
10	600 (272)	1-2	30 x 37 (76 x 94)	90 (806)

INCREASE TURNOVER AND DECREASE LEAD TIME
CIPET MOULD BASES - (CMB SERIES)

Dimension	**Code No.**									
	CMB 2020	**CMB** 2025	**CMB** 2030	**CMB** 2525	**CMB** 2530	**CMB** 2535	**CMB** 2540	**CMB** 3030	**CMB** 3035	**CMB** 3540
X	200	200	200	250	250	250	250	300	300	350
Y	200	250	300	250	300	350	400	300	350	400
X1	158	208	258	200	250	300	350	250	250	350
Y1	97	97	97	134	184	234	284	184	234	284
X2	98	98	98	128	128	128	128	178	178	300
Y2	168	218	268	218	268	318	368	268	318	368
X3	58	58	58	94	144	184	234	134	184	230
X4	120	120	120	150	150	150	150	200	200	250
T08	26	26	26	26	26	26	26	26	26	26
T07	16	16	16	26	26	26	26	26	26	
T06	12	12	12	16	16	16	16	16	16	16
T05	46*	46*	56*	66*	66*	66*	76*	76*	76*	86*
T04	36	36	36	36	36	36	36	46	46	46
T03	26*	36*	36*	36*	46*	46*	46*	46*	56*	56*
T02	26*	26*	36*	36*	36*	36*	46*	46*	46*	56*
T01	26	26	26	26	26	26	26	26	26	26

Note :- *Subject to Change as per the Requirement

PLEASE ALSO REFER PAGE NO. 146 OF THIS BOOK

T16	DOWEL PIN	2	STD	Ø12X L	-
T15	SOCKET HEAD SCREW	4	STD	M8(M10)X L	-
T14	SOCKET HEAD SCREW	4	STD	M12XL	-
T13	SOCKET HEAD SCREW	4	STD	M12XL	-
T12	PUSH BACK REST PIN	4	EN18		40-45 Rc
T11	PUSH BACK PIN	4	EN18		40-45 Rc
T10	GUIDE BUSH	3+1	EN18	FOR	40-45 Rc
T09	GUIDE PILLAR	3+1	EN18	SIZES,	40-45 Rc
T08	EJECTOR PLATE	1	EN2A	REFER	-
T07	EJECTOR BACK PLATE	1	EN2A	TABLE -1	-
T06	EJECTION-SIDE BACK PLATE	1	EN2A	&	-
T05	SPACER BLOCK	1SET	EN2A	ANNEXURE-2	-
T04	CORE BACK PLATE	1	EN2A		-
T03	CORE RETAINER PLATE	1	EN2A		-
T02	CAVITY RETAINER PLATE	1	EN2A		-
T01	INJECTION SIDE BACK PLATE	1	EN2A		-
DETAIL					
No.	DESCRIPTION	NO.OFF	MATERIAL	SIZE	HARDNESS

STANDARD MOULD PARTS

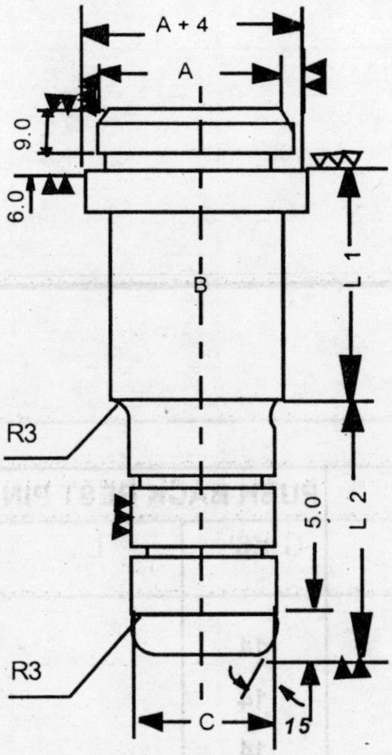

GUIDE PILLAR

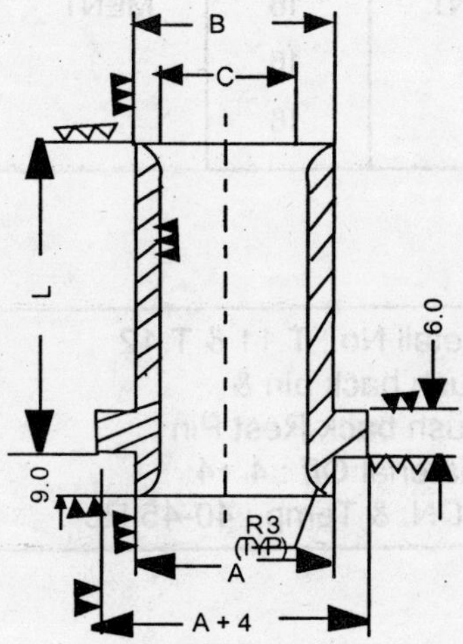

GUIDE BUSH

Code N.	A'j6'	B 'k6'	C 'g6'	L1	L2
CMB 2020	ø28	ø28	ø20		
CMB 2025	ø28	ø28	ø20		
CMB 2030	ø28	ø28	ø20		
CMB 2525	ø32	ø32	ø24	TO SUIT AS	
CMB 2530	ø32	ø32	ø24	PER THE	
CMB 2535	ø32	ø32	ø24	REQUIREMENT	
CMB 2540	ø32	ø32	ø24		
CMB 3030	ø32	ø32	ø24		
CMB 3052	ø32	ø32	ø24		
CMB 3540	ø32	ø32	ø24		

Code no.	A'j6'	B 'k6'	C'H7'	L
CMB 2020	ø28	ø28	ø20	
CMB 2025	ø28	ø28	ø20	
CMB 2030	ø28	ø28	ø20	
CMB 2525	ø32	ø32	ø24	
CMB 2530	ø32	ø32	ø24	To Suit As
CMB 2535	Ø32	Ø32	Ø24	Per The
CMB 2540	Ø32	Ø32	Ø24	Requirement
CMB 3030	Ø32	Ø32	Ø24	
CMB 3035	Ø32	Ø32	Ø24	
CMB 3540	Ø32	Ø32	Ø24	

Detail No. : T 09 & T 10
Guide Pillar & Guide Bush
Material : EN 18
Number Off : 3 + 1 (U/S)
HDN. & Temp. : 40-45 Rc

12

STANDARD MOULD PARTS

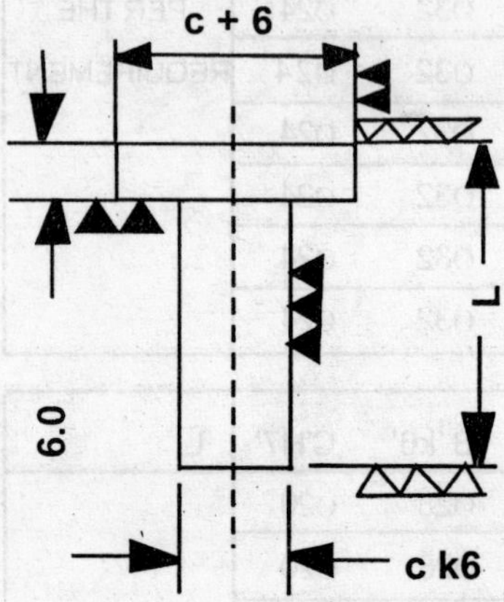

PUSH BACK REST PIN

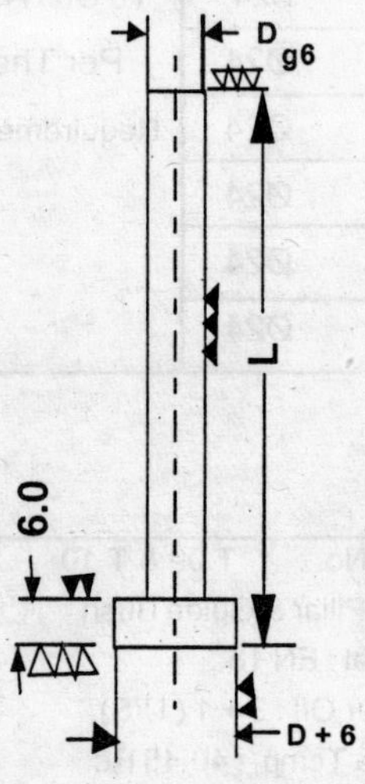

PUSH BACK PIN

CODE NO.	SIZE			
	PUSH BACK PIN		PUSH BACK REST PIN	
	D 'g6'	L	C 'K6'	L
CMB 2020	12	TO SUIT AS PER THE REQUIRE-MENT	14	TO SUIT AS PER THE REQUIRE-MENT
CMB 2025	12		14	
CMB 2030	12		14	
CMB 2525	14		16	
CMB 2530	14		16	
CMB 2535	14		16	
CMB 2540	14		16	
CMB 3030	14		16	
CMB 3035	14		16	
CMB 3540	14		16	

Detail No.: T 11 & T 12
push back pin &
Push back Rest Pin
Material Off : 4 +4
HDN. & Temp.: 40-45 Rc

SOCKET HEAR SCREWS CMB SERIES

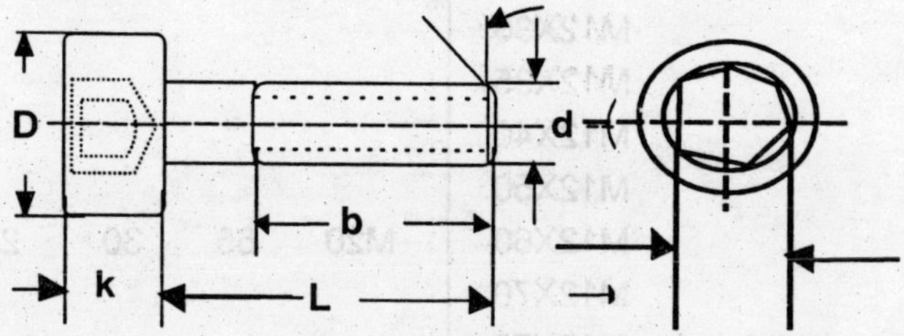

d	b	D	k	s	L
M4	12	7	4	3	M4X10
					M4X20
					M4X30
M5	15	9	5	4	M5X10
					M5X16
					M5X20
					M5X25
					M5X35
M6	18	10	6	5	M6X12
					M5X16
					M6X20
					M6X25
					M6X30
					M6X35
					M6X40
					M6X45
					M6X50
					M6X60
					M6X70
					M6X80
					M6X100
M8	22	13	8	6	M8X16
					M8X18
					M8X20
					M8X25

d	b	D	k	s	L
					M8X30
					M8X50
					M8X60
					M8X70
					M8X80
					M8X90
					M8X100
					M8X120
					M8X160
					M8X200
M10	25	16	10	8	M10X25
					M10X30
					M10X40
					M10X45
					M10X45
					M10X50
					M10X60
					M10X70
					M10X80
					M10X100
					M10X110
					M10X120
					M10X140
					M10X160
M12	28	18	12	10	M12X25

d	b	D	k	s	L
					M12X30
					M12X35
					M12X40
					M12X50
					M12X60
					M12X70
					M12X75
					M12X80
					M12X90
					M12X100
					M12X120
					M12X130
					M12X140
					M12X150
					M12X160
					M12X180
					M12X200
M16	38	24	16	14	M16X30
					M16X40
					M16X45
					M16X50
					M16X60
					M16X80
					M16X100
					M16X120
M16	44	24	16	14	M16X130
					M16X140
					M16X150
					M16X160
					M16X180
M16	57	24	16	14	M16X200
					M16X210
					M16X220
					M16X240
M20	52	30	20	17	M20X60

d	b	D	k	s	L
					M20X120
					M20X150
					M20X160
					M20X180
M20	65	30	20	17	M20X200
					M20X210
					M20X210
					M20X240
					M20X250

STANDARD DOWEL PINS

CNB SERIES DETAIL NO.:J16

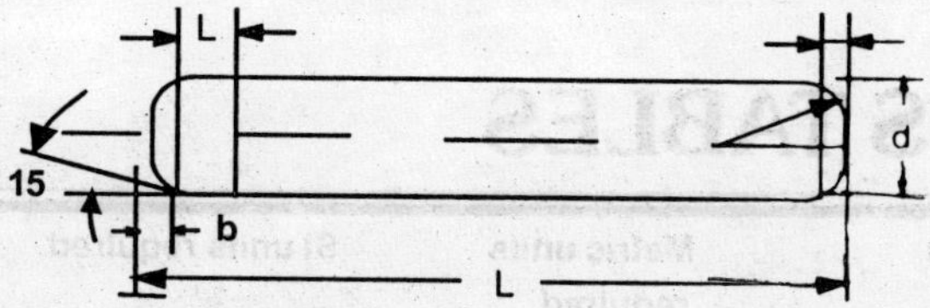

d	L_2	L_1	b	r	L
⌀3	0.8	0.45	0.3	3	10
					12
					16
					20
					28
⌀4	1	0.6	0.4	4	12
					16
					20
					24
					32
					40
⌀5	1.2	0.75	0.5	5	12
					16
					20
					24
					28
					32
					40
					45
					50
⌀6	1,5	0.9	0.6	6	16
					24
					32
					36
					40
					45
					50
					60
⌀8	1.8	1.2	0.8	8	20
					28
					32

d	L_2	L_1	b	r	L
					36
					40
					50
					60
⌀10	2	1.5	1	10	24
					32
					40
					50
					60
					80
⌀12	2.5	1.8	1.3	12	32
					40
					50
					60
					80
					90
					100
⌀14	2,5	2	1.3	16	40
					50
					70
					90
⌀14	2.5	2	1.3	16	120
⌀16	3	2.5	1.7	16	50
					80
					100
					120
					140
⌀20	4	3	2	20	60
					80
					100
					160

13

CONVERSIONS TABLES

Units Given in	English units irequired	Metric units required	SI units required	Usage
Fahrenheit	(Met x 1.8) + 32	-	-	1. Processing Temp. 2. Melting Point 3. Vicat Softening point 4. Brittleness Temp
Centigrade		(Eng-32) x 0.5555	-	4. Brittleness Temp 5. Deflection Temp
lb/ft^3	-	Eng x 0.01062	Eng x 16.02	Density
g/cm^3	Met x 62.43	-	Met x 1000	
kg/cm^3	SI x 0.06243	SI x 0.0010	-	
lb/ft^3	-	Eng x 0.07030	Eng x 6895	1. Tensile Strength 2. Tensile Modulus
kg/cm^2	Met x 14.22	-	Met x 98100	3. Flexural strength
Pa	SI x 0.0001450	SIxo.00001020	-	4. Flexural Modulus 5. Compressive Strength
ft.lb/in	-	Eng x 5.440	Eng x 0.05339	Izod Notched
kg cm/cm	Met x 0.1838	-	Met x 0.009810	
kJ/m	SI x 18.73	SI x 101.9	-	
BTU in/hr ft^2 ^0F	-	Eng x 0.000345	Eng x 0.1441	Thermal Conductivity
cal cm/sec cm^2 ^0C	Met x 2899	-	Met x 418.7	
W/m ^0K	SI x 6.940	SI x 0.0002388	-	
in/in^{0}F	-	Eng x 1. 80	Eng x 1.80	Linear Thermal expansion
cm/cm^{0}C	Met x 0.5555	-	Met	
m/m^{0}K	SI x 0.5555	SI	-	
v/10^{-3} in	-	Eng x 39.37	Eng x 39370	Dielectric strenght
v/mm	Met x 0.02540	-	Met x 1000	
v/m	SI x 0.00002540	SI x 0.0010	-	

Eng = Given English Units
Met = Given Metric Units
SI = Given SI units

Commonly Used Metric Conversions

Area

1	inch^2	in^2	=	645.6 mm^2
1	inch^2	in^2	=	0.000 645 m^2
1	foot^2	ft^2	=	0.0929 m^2
1	yard^2	yd^2	=	0.836 m^2

Density

1	gram per cc	g/cc	=	0.036 1 lb/in^3
1	pound per cu ft	lb/ft^3	=	16.02 kg/m^3
1	pound per cu ft	lb/ft^3	=	62.37 g/cc
1	pound per cu in	lb/in^3	=	0.027 7 kg/m^3

Electrical

1	volt per mil	V/mil	=	25.4 kV/mm

Energy-Work

1	erg	dyn.cm	=	1 x 10^{-7}J
1	Newton-meter	N.m	=	1 J
1	watt-second	W.s	=	1.J
1	foot-pound	ft.lbf	=	1.356 J
1	horsepower-hour	hph	=	2.685 x 10^6 J
1	kilowatt-hour	kWh	=	3.6 10^6 J
1	calorie	cal	=	4.19 J
1	British thermal unit	Btu	=	1,055 J
1	British thermal unit	Btu	=	0.000 11 cal
1	inch pound	in.lbf	=	0.133 J

Force

1	dyne	dyn	=	1 x 10^{-5} N
1	kilogram-force	kgf	=	9.81 N
1	pound force	lbf	=	4.448 N
1	ton-force	tf	=	9,810 N

Impact Strength

1	foot pound per inch^2	ft.lb/in^2	=	0.475 5 kj/m^2
1	foot pound per inch of notch (Izod test)	ft. lb/in.	=	0.01873 J/m

Length

1	kilometer	km	=	1,000 m
1	centimeter	cm	=	0.01 m

1	millimeter	mm	=	0.001 m
1	micron	um	=	1×10^{-6} m
1	nanometer	nm	=	1×10^{-9} m
1	Angstrom unit	A	=	1×10^{-10}m
1	inch	in	=	0.025 4m
1	foot	ft	=	0.304 8m
1	yard	yd	=	0.914 4m
1	mile	mile	=	1.609 m
1	inch/inch per ^{0}F	in./in./ ^{0}F	=	0.5567 mm/mm/^{0}C

Mass

1	gram	g	=	0.001 kg
1	ounce	oz	=	28.4 g
1	pound	lb	=	0.453 6 kg
1	ton	t	=	1,000 kg
1	ton	tn	=	907 kg
1	ton Uk	ton	=	1,016 kg

Power

1	kilowatt	kW	=	1,000 W
1	horsepower	hp	=	746 W
1	foot pound per second	ft.lbf/s	=	1.356

Specific Energy

1	calorie per gram	cal/gm	=	4,190 J/kg
1	Btu per pound	Btu	=	2,326 J/kg
1	hph per pound	hph/lb	=	5.92×10^6 J/kg
1	kWh per kg	kWh/kg	=	3.6×10^6 J/kg
1	kWh per kg	kWh	=	1.644 hph/lb

Stress

1	dyne per cm^2	dyn/cm^2	=	0.1 Pa
1	Newton per meter^2	N/m^2	=	1 Pa
1	Joule per meter^3	J/m^3	=	1 Pa
1	atmosphere	atm	=	1.013×10^5 Pa
1	mm mercury	mm Hg	=	133. . Pa
1	mm water	mm H_2O	=	9.81 Pa
1	bar	bar	=	1×10^5 Pa
1	pound per inch^2	psi	=	6,890 Pa
1	megapascal	MPa	=	145 psi
1	ton per inch^2	tn/in^2	=	140.7 kg/cm^2

Temperature

1	degree Fahrenheit	^0F	=	$1.8^0C + 32$
1	degree Celsius	^0C	=	$0.5555 (^0F.32)$
1	degree Kelvin	K	=	$^0C + 273.16)$
1	degree Rankine	^0R	=	$^0F + 459.69$

Thermal Conductivity

1	$cal/cm.s.^0C$		=	419 J/ms.K
1	$Kcal/m.h.^0C$		=	1.163 J/ms.K
1	$Btu/ft.hr.^0F$		=	0.144 J/ms.K
1	$Btu/ft^2.h.^0F$		=	0.144 J/ms.K
1	$Btu/ft.s.^0F$		=	6,230 J/ms.K
1	Wm.k		=	1 J/ms.K

Viscosity

1	Poise	Poise	=	0.1 Pa.s
1	Poise	Poise	=	$14.5x 10^{-6}$ psi.s
1	Poise	Poise	=	$1 dyn/cm^2$
1	$Poise-second/in^2$	psi.s	=	6,897 Pa.s

Volume

1	cubic centimeter	cc	=	$1 x 10^{-6}m^3$
1	liter	L	=	$0.001 m^3$
1	milliliter	mL	=	$1 x 10^{-6}m^3$
1	cubic inch	in^3	=	$1.639 x 10^{-5}m^3$
1	cubit foot	ft3	=	$0.028 32 m^3$
1	gallon US	gal Us	=	$0.003 785 m^3$
1	gallon UK	gal UK	=	$0.004 546 m^3$

A	=	Angstom Unit	g	=	Gram	MPa	=	Megapascal
atm	=	Atmosphere	h	=	Hour	N	=	Newton
But	=	British Thermal Unit	Hg	=	Mercury	oz	=	Ounce
C	=	Degrees Celsuis	Hp	=	Horspower	pa	=	Pascal
cal	=	calorie	in.	=	Inch	psi	=	Pounds per Square Inch
cc	=	Cubic Centimeter	J	=	Joule	R	=	Degrees Rankine
cm	=	Centimer	K	=	Degrees Kelvin	s	=	second
cu	=	Cubic	kg	=	Kilogram	t	=	Ton
f	=	Force	L	=	Liter	tn	=	Ton Us
dyn	=	Dyne	lb	=	Pound	ton	=	Ton Uk
F	=	Degrees Farenheit Force	m	=	Meter	v	=	Volts
ft	=	Foot	mL	=	Milliliter	w	=	Walt
gal	=	Gallon	mm	=	Millimeter	yd	=	Yard

CONVERSION FACTORS

Quantity	Si Unit	c.g.s. unit	f.p.s. or other
Length	1 m	100 cm	3.281 ft=39.37 in
Time	1 s	1 s	1 s
Mass	1 kg	1000 g	2.205 lb
Area	1 m^2	10^4 cm^2	1.764ft^2 = 1550.0 in^2
Volume	1 m^3	10^6 cm^3	35.31 ft^3 = 6.102 x 10^4 in^3
Frequency	1 Hz	1 c/s	1 c.p.s.
Rotational frequency	1 s^{-1}	1 rev/s	60 r.p.m.
Density	1 Mg/m^3	1 g/cm^3	62.43 lb/ft^3 = 0.03613 lb/in^3
Velocity	1 m/s	100 cm/s	3.281 ft/s = 39.37 in/s
Fluid velocity	1 m^3/s cm^3 /s	6 x 10^4 litres/min = 10^6	2119 ft^3 /min = 6. 1 x 10^4 in^3 /s
Force	1 N	1.102 kgf = 10^5 dynes	0.2248 lbf = 7.233 pdl
Surface tension	1 mN/m	1 dyne/cm	
Pressure*	1 MPa	10.20 kgf/cm^2= 10^7 dyne/cm^2	145 p.s.i.
Stress	1 kPa	10.20 gf/cm2 = 10^4 dyne/cm^2	0.1450 p.s.i.
Strength	1 Pa	7.5 x 10^{-3} mmHg	
Modulus	1 mN/m^2	7.5 x 10^{-6} mmHg	
Torque	1 Nm	10.20 kgf cm	141.6 oz in
Energy	1 J	1.019 x 10^4 gf cm = 0.239 cal = 0.239 cal = 10^7 ergs	0.738 ft lbf = 9.48 x 10^{-4} Btu
1 M		0.278 kWh = 239 kcal	948 Btu
Power 1 W	0.860 kcal/h	0.00134 HP = 3.41 Btu/h	
Momentum	1 kg m s^{-1}	10^5 g cms^{-1}	7.2307 lb ft s^{-1}
Moment of inertia	1 kg/m^2	107_g cm^2	23.730 lb ft^2
Thermal Conductivity	1 W/mk	0.00239 cal/cm^0Cs	6.93 Btu in/ft^2 ^{0}F h
viscosity - dynamic	1 Ns/m^2	10 poise	0.02089 lbf s ft^2
viscosity - kinematic	1 m^2 /s	10^4 stokes	
permeability	1 m^4/ Ns	1.0113 x $10^9$$cm^2$ /At s	
electrical resistivity	1 ohm	100 ohm	

* Pressure may also be expressed in bars (b)
1 bar = 10^5N/m^2 = 14.504 p.s.i.
+ Electrical, mecanical or heat energy

COMPARATIVE HARDNESS SCALES FOR POLYMERS

Brinell	Rockwell M	Rockwell a (= R)	Rockwell D	Shore C	Shore A (= IRHD*)	Types of product
25	100					**Hard plastics**
16	80					
12	70	100	90			
10	65	97	86			
9	63	96	83			**Moderately**
8	60	93	80			**hard**
7	57	90	77			**plastics**
6	54	88	74			
5	50	85	70			
4	45		65	95		
3	40		60	93	98	**Soft**
2	32		55	89	96	**plastics**
1.5	28		50	80	94	
1	23		42	70	90	
0.8	20		38	65	88	**Rubbers**
0.6	17		35	57	85	
0.5	15		30	50	80	
			25	43	75	
			20	36	70	
			15	27	60	
			12	21	50	
			10	18	40	
			8	15	30	
			6.5	11	20	
			4	8	10	

* IRHD = International rubber hardness degrees

MOULD BASES - (CMB SERIES)

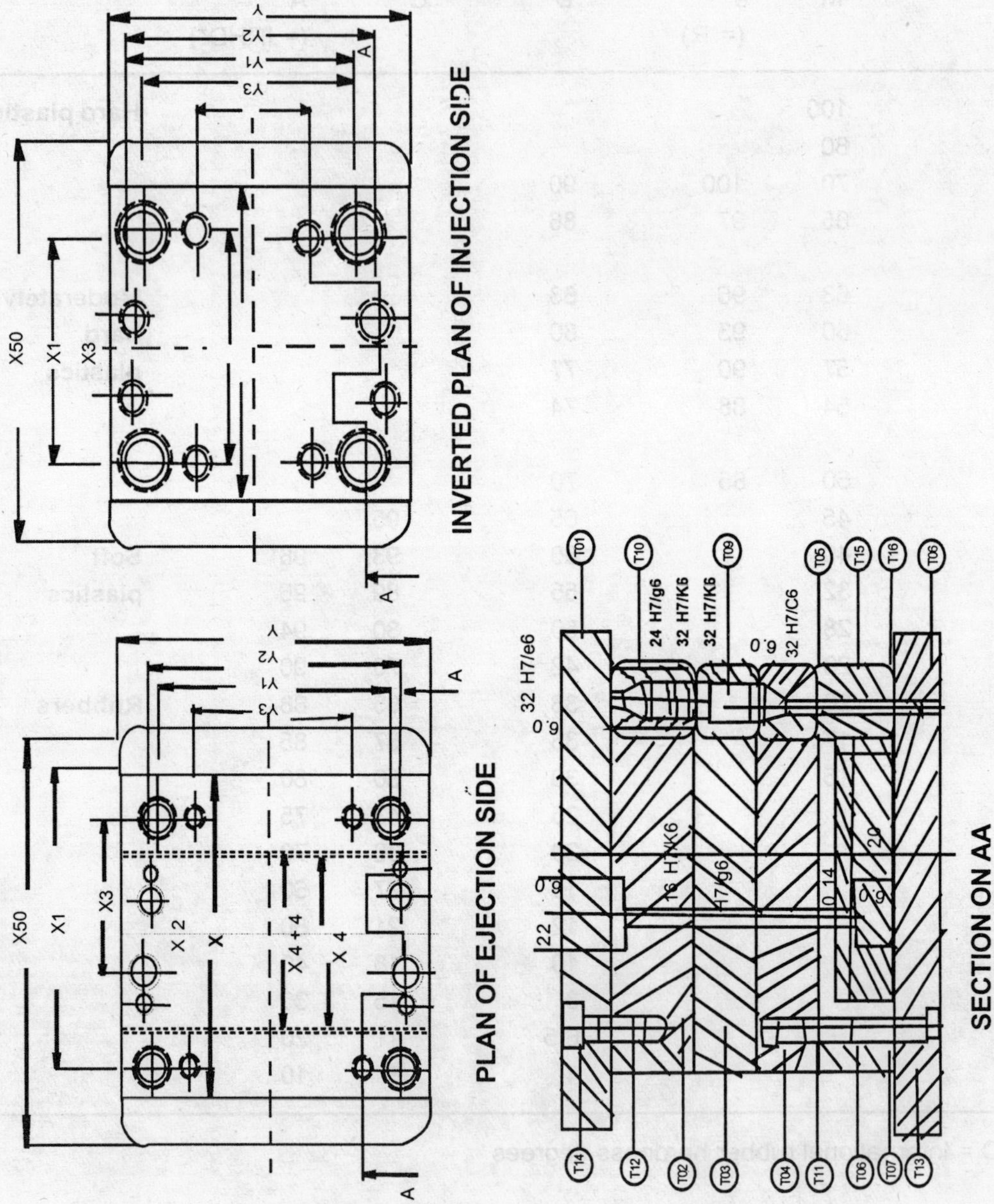

PLEASE ALSO REFER PAGE NO. 133 OF THIS BOOK

Brief Contents Covered in each

MARKET SURVEY CUM DETAILED TECHNO ECONOMIC FEASIBILITY REPORT

- Introduction
- Uses & Applications
- Market Position
- Installed Capacity
- Production and anticipated Demand Estimates
- Demand Supply Gap
- Detailed manufacturing Process
- Process Flow Sheet Diagram
- Raw Materials requirement
- Suppliers of Raw Materials
- Detailed Specifications of Machineries Required
- Land area with Rates
- Covered area breakup with costs of construction
- Plant Lay Out
- Plant & Machineries
- Staff Salaries & Wages
- Power, water & fuels
- Total Cost of Project
- Capital Investment
- Sources of Finance
- Profitability Analysis
- Break Even Point
- Depreciation Chart
- Repayment Chart
- Cash Flow Statement
- Projected Balance Sheet
- Land man ratio

AUTOMOBILES, MECHANICAL & METALLURGICAL

1. AGRICULTRAL EQUIPMENT
2. AGRICULTRAL EQUIPMENT INCLUDING THRESHERS
3. AIR BRAKE HELICAL COIL
4. AIR COOLER
5. AIR FILTERS(FOR SCOOTER CAR & EXCAVATORS ETC.)
6. ALUMINIUM ALLOY WHEELS
7. ALUMINIUM ALLOYS FROM ALUMINIUM SCRAP TO MAKE UTENSILS (INDUCTION FURNACE)
8. ALUMINIUM BOTTLE MANUFACTURING (COLD EXTRUSION OF ALUMINIUM)
9. ALUMINIUM CANS FOR BEER PACKAGING
10. ALUMINIUM EXTRUSION
11. ALUMINIUM SHEET ROLLING MILL
12. ALUMINIUM UTENSILS
13. ALUMINIUM UTENSILS & SCHOOL BOXES
14. ALUMINIUM WIRE DRAWING AND SUPER ENAMELLING FOR WINDING
15. ANODISED ALUMINIUM UTENSILS
16. ANODIZING OF ALUMINIUM
17. ANTIMONY OXIDE FROM LEAD SCRAP
18. ARC WELDING FILTER GLASS
19. AUTO FLAPS FOR TRUCKS & BUSES
20. AUTO GEARS
21. AUTO HORNS
22. AUTO LEAF SPRING
23. AUTO TUBES
24. AUTO PISTON RING
25. BALL POINT PEN REFILLS
26. BALL ROLLER & TAPER BEARING
27. BAND SAW BLADES
28. BARBED WIRE
29. BICYCLE SPOKES
30. BRASS CASTING
31. BRIGHT BARS
32. BUFFING AND POLISHING INDUSTRY (JOB WORK)
33. BUTT HINGE (BRASS SHEET)
34. CARBON BRUSH HOLDER & SLIP RING
35. CO_2 WELDING WIRE ELECTRODES (COPPER/ COPPER ALLOY COATED M.S.WIRE)
36. CARBON FILM RESISTORS
37. CARBURETTORS
38. CAST STEEL PANES FOR MELTING FURNACE
39. CHEMICAL ETCHING OF STAINLESS STEEL
40. CHEMICAL RESISTANT IRON & STEEL
41. COLD FORM SECTION MILL
42. COLD ROLLED FORMING OF SECTION AND OTHER SECTIONS
43. COLD ROLLING OF MS STRIP
44. COLD TWISTED DE-FORMED RIBBED STEEL
45. CONTINUOUSLY CAST STEEL WIRE RODS (5 mm)
46. CONVEYOR BELTINGS
47. CONVEYOR BELT, TRANSM -ISSION BELT & V BELTS
48. COOKING RANGES
49. COPPER/BRASS SHEETS, CIRCLE & UTENSILS
50. COPPER FOIL
51. COPPER PRODUCTS FROM COPPER SCRAP
52. COPPER SMELTING PLANT
53. COPPER WIRE RODS FROM COPPER SCRAP
54. CYLINDER LINER FOR AUTOMOBILES
55. DOOR LOCKS/PAD LOCKS
56. DRILL BITS & TOOL BITS
57. DRUM CLOSURES
58. ERW STEEL CONDUIT PIPE
59. EARTH MOVING EQPT.
60. ENGINE VALVES FOR AUTOMOBILES
61. FABRICATION OF HEAT EXCHANGER
62. FABRICATION OF STORAGE TANKS AND M.S. DRUM
63. FERROUS ALLOY NI-HARDY I.V CASTING
64. FERROUS Mn ALLOY CASTING BY ALUMINA THERMIC PROCESS
65. FIRE EXTINGUISHERS
66. FLIP-TONE CANS
67. FORGED CONECTING ROD
68. FORGING UNIT
69. FOUNDRY SAND
70. FUEL INJECTION SYSTEM
71. GALVANIZED M.S.STRIPS
72. GALVANIZED IRON WIRE
73. GAS WELDING TORCHES AND NOZZLES
74. GASKET SHEET
75. GATE GRILLS & WINDOW FRAMES
76. GENERATING SET (DIESEL)
77. HARD ANODISED ALUMINIUM
78. HOSPITAL WARES
79. HOSPITAL FURNITURES
80. HOT DIP GALVANIZING
81. HOT MIX PLANT
82. INVESTMENT CASTING
83. IRON/STEEL WIRE GAUGE
84. KNIVES (S.S.KNIVES)
85. KITCHEN SINK (S.S.)
86. L.P.G REGULATORS
87. MACHINE SCREWS & SELF TAPPING SCREWS
88. MARUTI WORKSHOP CUM SERVICE STATION
89. MAGNESIUM INGOTS & BULLETS CASTING
90. MANUFACTURE OF TIN CONTAINERS
91. MARK II HAND PUMPS
92. MARUTI WORKSHOP CUM-SERVICE STATION
93. MECHANICAL JACKS
94. METAL CUTTING DIE DESIGN
95. METAL CUTTING OF AND GRINDING WHEELS (ABRASIVE CUTTING WHEELS)
96. METAL HOOKS & CLIPS
97. METALLIC RING JOINTS
98. METALLIC GASKET (SPIRAL WOUND)
99. MICROVEE & ABSOLUTE FILTER
100. MICROWAVE OVEN
101. MILD STEEL INGOTS
102. MINI STEEL PLANT
103. MODERN VEHICLE WORKSHOP
104. MOPED
105. M.S.HINGES
106. M.S.INGOT AND HR. STEEL STRUCTURALS
107. M.S.INGOT BY INDUCTION FURNACES
108. M.S.PIPES
109. M.S. WELDING ELECTRODE
110. MUFFLERS & SILENCERS FOR THREE WHEELERS
111. NICHROME WIRE
112. NICKEL LINED SCREENS
113. NON-FERROUS ALLOY ROLLING
114. NON-FERROUS FORGING
115. NON-FERROUS FOUNDRY
116. NON PRESSURE
117. INCANDESCENT LAMP
118. NUMBER COMBINATION LOCKS FOR LUGGAGES
119. NUTS & BOLTS
120. PAPER COATED ALUMINIUM AND COPPER WIRE
121. PETROMAX CONTAINER
122. PHOTO ETCHING OF STAINLESS STEEL PLATES
123. PIPE GALVANIZING PLANT
124. PISTON RING-AUTOMOBILE
125. PLANT PROTECTION EQUIPMENTS
126. PLATINUM LABORATORY APPARATUS
127. PRESSURE COOKER & ALUMINIUM UTENSILS
128. PRESSURE DIE CASTING
129. PRINTED ALUMINIUM COLLAPSIBLE TUBES
130. PRINTED TIN CONTAINERS
131. PRINTING PRESS (CYLINDER MACHINE)
132. PUMPS FOR CHEMICAL INDUSTRY (SPECIAL)
133. RAILWAY SLEEPERS (M.S.)
134. RAZOR TWIN BLADE
135. R.C.C SPUN PIPES
136. RE-ROLLING COPPER AND BRASS SHEET AND RODS
137. RE-ROLLING MILLS
138. RESIN COATED SAND
139. RESIN CORED SOFT SOLDER WIRES
140. ROLLER BEARING AND FORGING
141. ROLLING OF STAINLESS STEEL PATTA
142. RUBBER INSULATED PLIERS (HAND TOOLS)
143. RUBBING COMPOUND FOR AUTOMOBILES
144. SCIENTIFIC LABORATORY EQUIPMENTS
145. SECONDARY LEAD EXTRAC-TION BY SCRAP BATTERY PLATES,PIPES & SHEET
146. SEAMLESS M.S. TUBES & PIPES
147. SELF TAPPING STEEL SCREW
148. SEWING NEEDLES
149. S.G. IRON & ALLOY STEEL

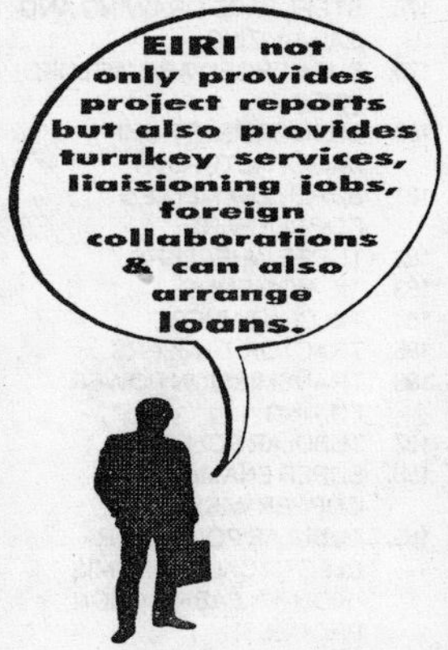

Apart from the above mentioned reports EIRI is also having other most lucrative projects (as many as 30,000). You just name it and we have that report

602. TRANSMISSION POWER LINE FITTING
603. TRANSMISSION TOWER FITTING
604. TV AUDIO EQUIPMENT CABINETS & THEIR ASSEMBLING UNIT
605. UN-INTERRUPTED POWER SUPPLY (U.P.S)
606. VARIABLE FREQUENCY
607. VARIABLE VOLTAGE A.C. DRIVE
608. VIDEO CASSETTES (COMPLETE MANUFACTURING AND ASSEMBLING)
609. VIDEO CASSETTES RECORDER (V.C.R)
610. VIDEO FILM STUDIO
611. VOLTAGE REGULATOR FOR AUTOMOBILES
612. VOLTAGE STABILIZERS
613. VOLTAGE STABLIZERS AND T.V. GAIN BOOSTER
614. WAX AND CHEMICAL COATED, BRAIDED TINSEL WIRE
615. WELDING ELECTRODES
616. WIND ENERGY POWER PROJECT (10 MW) WIRE WOUND POTENTIOMETERS

FOOD AND ALLIED PRODUCTS

617. ANTI SCALE COMPOUND FOR ADDING INTO SUGAR JUICE BOILING
618. APPLE JUICE CONCEN TRATED & DEHYDRATED FRUIT & VEGETABLES
619. ARTIFICIAL FISH MEAL FOR POULTRY FEED
620. AUTOMATIC BISCUIT PLANT
621. BABY CEREAL FOOD AND MILK POWDER
622. BACTERIA FOR CANE JUICE
623. BAKER'S YEAST
624. BAKERY INDUSTRY
625. BANANA PUREE
626. BEER & WINE
627. BEER PLANT (BREWERY)
628. BREAD (AUTOMATIC PLANT)
629. BLACK PEPPER (SPICES)
630. BREAD AND BISCUITS
631. BREEDING FARM
632. BUTTON MUSHROOM CULTIVATION & PROCESSING
633. CAFFEIN FROM TEA WASTE
634. CANNING OF FRUITS & VEGETABLES
635. CASEIN AND BY-PRODUCTS
636. CASHEWNUT KERNEL EXTRACTION FROM CASHEWNUT FRUIT
637. CASHEWNUT SHELL LIQUID AND KERNEL PROCESSING
638. CASHEW FENI
639. CATECHEU (BY CHEMICAL PROCESS)
640. CATTLE FEED FROM TAPIOCA
641. CHEWING & BUBBLE GUM
642. CHICKEN/SHEEP MEAT PROCESSING
643. CHOCOLATE (MILK)
644. CIGARETTE AND BEEDIES
645. COCOA BUTTER FROM COCOA MASS
646. COCONUT PROCESSING UNIT (INTEGRATED PLANT)
647. COLD/SOFT DRINKS
648. COLLECTION OF MILK AND MILK MAKING POWDER
649. COLLECTION OF MILK AND PACKING IN POLYTHENE POUCH (1/2 KG.1 KG. & 2 KG.)
650. CONDENSED MILK (SWEETNED)
651. CONFECTIONERY INDUSTRY (TOFFEE & CANDY, SEMI-AUTOMATIC PLANT)
652. COUNTRY LIQUOR FROM MOLASSES
653. DAIRY FARM AND DAIRY (MILK) PRODUCTS (PASTEURISED MILK, BUTTER, GHEE, PANEER)
654. DAIRY FARM TO PRODUCE MILK & PACKING IN POUCHES (50%) & CAN(50%)
655. DAIRY FOR MILK PROCESSING
656. DAIRY FARM (BUFALO)
657. DAL (PULSE) MILL UNIT
658. DEHYDRATION OF CARROT & GARLIC
659. DEHYDRATION OF FRUITS AND VEGETABLES
660. DEHYDRATED ONIONS AND ONION POWDER
661. DRY ICE BY BREAKING OF AIR
662. DRYING OF RED CHILLIS, HALDI, DHANIA, AND GREEN PEAS
663. EGG POWDER (40,000 EGGS PROCESSING PER DAY)
664. EXPORT OF PROCESSED FOODS AND MARINE PRODUCTS
665. FISH CANNING & POUCHING
666. FISH FARMING (PRAWN & OTHER MARINE PRODUCTS)
667. FISH MEAL
668. FLOUR MILL AND MUSTARD OIL
669. FOOD COLOUR & ORASTED GROUNDNUT GRAM PEAS, ETC IN POUCHES
670. FROG LEGS PROCESSING
671. FROZEN MEATS PROCESSING
672. FOOD FLAVOURS (WHISKY) VODKA, GRAPE, BUTTER SCOTCH)
673. FRUIT JUICE, JAM, JELLIES & ALLIED PRODUCTS
674. FRUIT JUICE, PICKLES PROCESSING AND CANNING
675. FRUIT JUICE MAKING AND PACKING IN PLASTIC CONTAINER/POUCHES
676. FRUIT PROCESSING (JAM & JELLIES)
677. FRUIT PULP & JUICE CONCENTRATES
678. FRUIT & VEGETABLE DRYING (FREEZE DRYING METHOD)
679. GOAT & SHEEP FARMING
680. GRAM DALL/PULSE MILL
681. GRAPE DEHYDRATION
682. HARD BOILED CANDY (TOFFEE & CANDY)
683. HERBAL CIGARETTES
684. HONEY PROCESSING AND PACKAGING
685. ICE CREAM OF DIFFERENT FLAVOURS
686. ICE CREAM STABILIZER
687. ICE MAKING PLANT
688. INDIAN MADE FOREIGN LIQUOR (I.M.F.L)
689. INSTANT FOOD (IDLI MIX, DOSA MIX, GULAB JAMUN MIX)
690. INSTANT FOOD (INSTANT FOOD+FAST FOOD PARLOUR)
691. INSTANT NOODLES
692. INSTANT TEA
693. INSTANT TEA FROM BLACK TEA
694. INTEGERATED STARCH BAKING POWDER/YEAST INDUSTRY
695. IODIZED SALT
696. IODIZED SALT (ORDINARY MOISTURE-LESS/FREE FLOWING IN PLASTIC BAGS AND CONTAINERS)
697. JAM, JELLIES, FRUIT JUICE & ALLIED PRODUCTS
698. KATHA AND CUTCH
699. KHANDSARI SUGAR
700. KHANDSARI SUGAR & IMFL
700A. LACTIC ACID FROM WHITE SUGAR BY FERMENTATION PROCESS
701. LACTOSE & BY PRODUCTS PROCESSING FROM MILK
702. LIQUID GLUCOSE AND ITS BYE PRODUCTS
703. MACRONI AND VERMICILLI
704. MALT EXTRACTION FROM BARLEY
705. MANGO PROCESSING (MANGO PULP, JUICE & SLICES)
706. MAYUR BRAND TYPE CHEWING TOBACCO
707. MINERAL WATER
708. MILK PRESERVATION & MARKETING TO WHOLE SELLERS (INPOUCH PACKING BY UHT TECHNOLOGY)
709. MILK PROCESSING AND PACKAGING OF MILK PRODUCTS
710. MILK PRODUCTS (CASEIN, LACTOSE, GHEE & WHEY POWDER)
711. MILK TOFFEE
712. MINI FLOUR MILL
713. MINI SUGAR PLANT
714. MISRI (PEARL SUGAR CANDIES)
715. MODERN RICE MILL
716. MURABBA
717. MUTTON TALLOW
718. NON-BASMATI RICE FROM PADDY
719. OLEORESIN, ESSENTIAL OIL, DYES & POWDER OF SPICES
720. OLEORESIN EXTRACTION FROM DIPTERO-CARPUT TURMINATUS AND PINUS KHASYANA
721. OLEORESIN EXTRACTION FROM CHILLI
722. PAN MASALA AND POUCH MAKING
723. PAN MASALA, TOBACCO, ZARDA & KIMAM
724. PANEER FROM MILK
725. PAPPAD PLANT
726. PAPAIN FROM PAPAYA (PAPAYA LATEX)
727. PECTIN FROM MANGO PEEL PECTIN FROM APPLE POMACE
728. PICKLES AND SAUCES
729. PICKLES MURABBA ETC. (VEG. & NON. VEG.PICKLES)
730. PIGGERY MEAT PROCESS
731. PINE-APPLE JUICE PREPARATION & PACKAGING
732. POTATO POWDER
733. POULTRY FEED
734. PROCESSED FOODS & SPICES (EOU)
735. PROCESSED READYMADE FOOD
736. PROCESSING OF FRUITS AND VEGETABLES
737. RASGULLAS MAKING AND CANNING IN METAL CANS
738. READY TO EAT SNACK

Price Rs. 3150/- for each "Detailed Project Report" Payable in advance through Draft/Cash/M.O. in favour of *"ENGINEERS INDIA RESEARCH INSTITUTE"*. 4449, Nai Sarak, Main Road Delhi - 110 006 *OR Ask by V.P.P.* • Ph : 391 8117, 391 6431, 392 0361, 396 0797 • Fax : 91-11-391 6431 E-Mail : eirisidi@bol.net.in

FOOD (CRAX, ROLL & BALL TYPE)
739. RICE AND CORN FLAKES
740. ROASTED/SALTED/ MASALACASHEW-NUTS, ALMONDS & PEANUTS
741. ROLLER FLOUR MILL
742. SALT LICKS FOR CATTLE
743. SAUSAGES FOOD CASING
744. SOFT DRINKS
745. SOFT DRINKS ESSENCES
746. SOFT DRINKS (NON CARBONATED) MANGO, LICCHI, PINEAPPLE FLAVOURS- FROOTI TYPE IN TETRAPACK)
747. SOFTY ICE CREAM CONES (FULLY AUTOMATIC)
748. SOYABEAN PRODUCTS
749. SOYA MILK & PANEER
750. STARCH & ALLIED PROPDUCTS FROM BROKEN RICE
751. SUGARCANE JUICE PRESERVATION
752. SUGAR CUBES FROM CANE SUGAR
753. SUGAR PLANT(Rs.30Cr.Proj.)
754. SWEET AROMA BETEL NUT
755. SYNTHETIC TALLOW
756. TAMARIND JUICE POWDER
757. TEA & COFFEE PROCESSING & PACKAGING
758. TOFFEES, GOLIES, CANDY (HARD BOILED)
759. TOMATO PRODUCTS
760. TUITY FRUITY
761. VODKA FROM POTATOES
762. WINE, BRANDY, WHISKY AND CHAMPAGNE
763. YEAST FROM MOLASSES
764. ZARDA, KIMAM NO. 60,90,120,160,240,300 & 400 (TOBACCO)
765. ZARDA-ZAFRANI (BABA-CHHAP TYPE)

GUMS & ADHESIVE

766. ACRYLIC ADHESIVE
767. ADHESIVE (FEVICOL TYPE)
768. ADHESIVE BASED ON POLYURETHANE
769. ADHESIVE FOR BAND AID (JOHNSON & JOHNSON TYPE)
770. ADHESIVE INDUSTRIES (LAMINATED, STICKER,DDL & OTHER TYPES)
771. ADHESIVE FOR GASKET (LIQUID/PASTE)
772. GUAR GUM
773. GUM BOTTLE (PVC)
774. GUM FOR PASTING LABELS
775. OFFICE PASTE
776. RUBBER ADHESIVE
777. SURGICAL ADHESIVE PLASTER

LEATHER & LEATHER PRODUCTS

778. HANDMADE LEATHER
779. LEATHER BOARD FROM LEATHER WASTE
780. LEATHER FOR UPHOLSTRY (SOFA)
781. LEATHER GARMENTS
782. LEATHER GOODS
783. LEATHER SHOES
784. LEATHER SHOE & CHAPPAL
785. LEATHER SUITCASES, BRIEFCASES AND TRAVELLING BAGS
786. LEATHER GOODS AND GARMENTS
787. SHEEP SKIN PICKLING PLANT
788. SHOE UPPER
789. SPORT SHOES (PLASTIC)

MISCELLANEOUS PRODUCTS

790. AGARBATTI (INSENCE STICK)
790A AGARBATTI (Mosquito Repellent)
790B AGARBATI BAMBOO STICK
791. AGARBATTI SYNTHETIC PERFUMERY COMPOUND
792. AIR FRESHNER(ODONIL TYPE)
793. AIR TAXI
794. AMUSEMENT PARK
795. ANODIC ALUMINIUM LABEL
796. AQUACULTURE PRAWN FARMING (100% EOU)
797. AQUA CULTURE SHRIMP FARMING (100% EOU)
798. ARTIFICIAL FLOWERS
799. ARTIFICIAL JEWELLERY
800. ASBESTOS YARN
801. ASH TRAYS FOR MARUTI VEHICLE
801A AIR BUBBLE PACKAGING
802. ASPHALTIC ROOFING SHEET (METAL COMPONENTS)
803. AUTOMATIC BOOK BINDING
803A ALKYD RESIN
803B APPLE JUICE CONCENTRATE
804. BALL POINT PEN FEFILLS (JOTTER TYPE)
805. BANK BRANCH BUILDING
806. BANQUET HALL
807. BIO-COAL BRIQUETTES FROM AGRICULTURAL CELLULOSE WASTE
808. BOOT CREAM/POLISH
809. BUFFING & POLISHING COMPOUND
810. BRASS BADGES BY ETCHING
811. BRIQUETTED FUEL FROM AGRO WASTE
812. BRIQUETTING OF LIGNITE COAL
813. BUFFALO HORN TIP, HOOF
813A BANQUET HALL
814. BUTTON
815. CALCINED PETROLEUM (C.P) COKE
816. CANVAS SHOES
817. CANVAS SHOES, JUNGLE BOOTS
818. CARBON BRUSH, BRUSH HOLDER AND SLIP RING
819. CEMENT SHEETS WITH COIR FIBRE AND OTHER SEGMENTS
820. CERAMIC TILES (GLAZED) BY DOUBLE FIRING/ HEATING
821. CINNAMON
822. COAL BRIQUETTES
823. COLD STORAGE & ICE
824. COLD STORAGE FOR FRUITS AND VEGETABLES
825. COSTUME JEWELLERY/ IMITATION JEWELLERY
826. DECORATIVE LAMINATED SHEET (SUNMICA)
827. DIAMOND CUTTING AND EXPORTING
828. DRINKING STRAW FROM PROPYLENE
829. FASHION TECHNOLOGY INSTITUTE
830. FAST FOOD PARLOUR
831. FAST FOOD (INSTANT FOOD & FAST FOOD PARLOUR)
832. FIRE EXTINGUISHERS (SODA ACID TYPE)
833. FISH NET
834. FLORICULTURE (CUT FLOWER ROSE) WITH GREEN HOUSE
835. FLOOR COVERING SHEET
835A FILM STUDIO (VIDEO)
836. FLUSH DOOR, CHIP BOARD, WOOD WOOL & OTHER INSULATING BOARDS
837. GAS DETECTORS OF L.P.G
837A. GEMS MANUFACTURING
838. GLASS BOTTLE BY SCRAP
839. GOAT & SHEEP FARMING
840. GOLD ELECTROPLATING
841. GOLD JEWELLERY (E.O.U)
842. GOLD PLATED SILVER JEWELLERY & CUTLERY
843. GRANITE SLAB AND TILES
844. GREEN HOUSE
845. HARD CHROMIUM PLATING
846. HEALTH CLUB AND BEAUTY PARLOUR CUM HAIR SALOON WITH SONA BATH
847. HEALTH CLUB CUM BEAUTY PARLOUR TRAINING INSTITUTE
848. HORN TIP,HOOVE BUTTON
849. HOSPITAL
850. HOSPITAL (100 BEDS)
851. HOSPITAL (200 BEDS)
852. ICE MAKING PLANT
853. IMITATION AND COSTUME
854. JEWELLERY (NECKLACE, EARRINGS EAR TOP ETC.)
855. INITMATE SCENT CHEMICAL FROM ALL TYPES OF FLAVOUR
856. INVESTMENT CASTING
857. JUTE, COIR, GLASS ROPE/ SUTLI
858. JUTE TWINE
859. L.P.G BOTTLING PLANT
860. L.P.G REGULATOR (DOMESTIC PURPOSE)
861. LAMINATED PARTICLE BOARD & HARD BOARD
862. LAMINATED SAFETY AND TOUGHENED GLASS
863. LEASING & HIRE PURCHASE
864. LICHEN (CHARILA)
865. MANILA ROPES
865A MEDICAL COLLEGE
866. MATCH UNIT FROM WAXED PAPER
867. MEDIUM DENSITY FIBRE BOARD
868. MELAMINE CROCKERY
869. MINERAL WATER
870. MINI CEMENT PLANT
871. MIRROR SILVER, GOLDEN, PINK, BLACK & SMOKES
872. MODERN ADVERTISING AGENCY WITH DTP & FILM STUDIO
873. MOTEL/SMALL HOTEL
874. MULTI COLOUR PRINTING
875. MULTI STOREY COMMERCIAL COMPLEX ALONGWITH RESIDENTIAL AND DELUX FLATS FOR FOREIGN TOURISTS & REVOLVING RESTAURENT AT THE TOP
876. MULTIPLE LAMINATION INDUSTRY
876A. MUSHROOM GROWING AND PROCESSING (BY DEEP FREEZING METHOD)
877. NEWS PAPER PRINTING
878. NICKEL LINED INDUSTRIAL SCREEN
879. OFFSET COLOUR PRINTING PRESS (SIX COLOUR)
880. OFFSET PRINTING PRESS
881. P.C.C ELECTRIC POLES
882. PHOTOGRAPHIC DEVEL -OPER & FIXER
882A PVC EXTRUSION PROFILE
882B POP- CORN
882C PHOTO ETCHING OF S.S.
883. PRE STRESSES CEMENT CONCRETE PIPES
884. PILFER PROOF CAPS
885. PILFER PROOF CAPS AND CROWN CAP
886. POUCH MAKING AND GRAVURE PRINTING
887. POULTRY AND FISH FARMING (INTEGERATED UNIT)
888. PRINTING OF TIN SHEETS
889. READYMADE GARMENTS
890. RESTAURANT
891. ROSE PLANTATION AND ROSE OIL EXTRACTION
892. ROTOGRAVURE PRINTING
893. SAFETY BELTS
894. SAFETY MATCHES
895. SHOE LACES
896. SILKCOCOON CULTIVATION (GROWING OF SILK COCOON WARM)
897. SILK SCREEN PRINTING FORMULATIONS FOR PLASTIC, PAPER & CLOTH
897A SPIKENARD (JATAMANSI)
898. STENCIL COATING SOLUTION
899. SUGAR CANDY (MISRI)
900. SUGAR CANE PLANTATION
901. SURAT ZARI
902. SYNTHETIC SHOES & SOLES
903. TEA PACKAGING INDUSTRY
904. TENNIS BALLS
905. THREE STAR HOTEL
906. TRAVELLING AGENCY

INFOTECH AND IT PROJECTS FROM EIRI DESK Rs. 3150/- EACH

1. E-COMMERCE/E-BUSINEES
2. PORTAL
3. INTERNET SERVICE PROVIDER
4. CYBER CAFE
5. MEDICAL TRANSCRIPTION
6. COMPUTER EDUCATION INSTITUTE
7. COMPUTER SOFTWARE
8. CALL CENTRE
9. E-SCHOOL
10. ON LINE SHOPPING MALL
11. INTERNET BASED STOCK TRADING
12. BACK OFFICE OPERATIONS
13. CYBERKIOSK
14. DATA PROCESSING CENTRE
15. FRANCHISEE COMPUTER EDUCATION CENTER
16. ON LINE SCHOOL (WEB BASED EDUCATION)
17. TRAINING INSTITUTE OF MEDICAL TRANSCRIPTION

1008. INFUSION & TRANSFUSION SETS (I.V. SET)
1009. INJECTABLE FOR PHARMACEUTICALS
1010. INJECTION AMPOULES PACKAGING BOX
1011. INTEGERATED SURGICAL COTTON
1012. ICE MAKING PLANT
1012A ICE & COLD STORAGE
1013. LACTOSE & BY PRODUCTS PROCESSING FROM MILK
1014. LICHEN (JATAMANSI CHARILA)
1015. LIQUID GLUCOSE AND ITS BY-PRODUCTS
1015A L-LYSINE MONOHYDRO CHLORIDE
1016. LIQUID GLUCOSE FROM POTATOES
1017. MEDICAL COLLEGE
1018. NICOTINE FROM TOBACCO WASTE
1019. PHARMACEUTICAL AND FOOD GRADE GELATINE
1020. PHARMACEUTICAL INDUSTRY (TABLETS, CAPSULES, LIQUID, GEL, OINTMENT POWDER INJECTABLE)
1021. PHARMACEUTICAL UNIT (EOU) WITH FORMULA TIONS, INJECTABLES, ETC. PYRIDINE AND DERIVATIVES
1021A SALT (IODIZED SALT)
1022. SALINE & INJECTION WATER
1023. SALINE WATER & DEXTROSE SOLUTION (I.V.FLUID IN PLASTIC BOTTLES)
1024. SORBITOL
1024A STARGH (MAIZE)
1025. SURGICAL ADHESIVE PLASTER
1027. SURGICAL BANDAGES
1027A SURGICAL GLOVES
1028. SURGICAL COTTON
1029. SURGICAL COTTON AND BANDAGE
1030. SYNTHETIC CAMPHOR POWDER
1031. TABLETS & CAPSULES
1032. TISSUE CULTURE
1033. TINCTURE FROM RECTIFIED SPIRIT
1034. TRIMETHOPIME
1035. VETERENARY MEDICINES (ONLY FORMULATIONS)
1036. VITAMIN 'C', SORBITOL' ANHYDROUS DEXTROSE, STARCH

PULP, PAPER & STATIONERY

1037. AMMONIA PAPER
1038. AUTOMATIC BOOK BINDING
1038A ADHESIVE (FEVICOL TYPE)
1039. ALL PIN & GEM CLIPS
1040. CARBON PAPER
1041. CARD BOARD
1042. CELLPHANE PAPER
1043. COMPUTER FORMS & SECURITY PRINTING PRESS
1044. CORRUGATED BOARD & BOX (PRINTED & LAMINATED)
1045. CORRUGATED BOARD AND BOXES FROM FROM CARD BOARDS
1046. CORRUGATED CARTONS FROM PLAIN PAPERS
1047. CORRUGATRED PACKING AND MATERIAL (BULB AND TUBES PACKING)
1048. DESK TOP PUBLISHING
1049. D.T.P CUM OFFSET PRESS
1050. EGG TRAYS
1051. EXERCISE NOTE BOOK, REGISTER AND PAD
1052. FLEXOGRAPHIC INK
1053. GREETING CARD BY OFFSET PRESS
1054. HAND MADE PAPER
1055. HARD BOARD
1056. INJECTION AMPOULES PACKAGING BOXES
1057. KRAFT PAPER
1058. KRAFT PAPER FROM BAGASSE
1059. LAMINATED PACKAGING PAPER WITH PRINTING
1059A LAMINATION & COATING ON PAPER
1060. M.G. PAPER FROM WASTE PAPER
1061. MILL PAPER FROM WASTE PAPER
1062. MILL BOARD FROM RICE AND WHEAT STRAWS
1063. MILL BOARD FROM WASTE PAPER
1064. MINI PAPER PLANT
1065. MULTI WALL PAPER SACKS
1066. NEWSPAPER FOR CHILDREN
1067. NEWS PRINT PAPER FROM RICE STRAW BAGASSE
1068. NEWS PAPER CHILDRENS (DAILY)
1069. NEWS PRINT PAPER
1070. OFFSET AND TREADLE TYPE PRINTING PRESS
1071. MILL BOARD BASED ON RICE STRAW
1072. PAPER AND BOARD FROM STRAW
1073. PAPER & PAPER PRODUCTS
1074. PAPER BAGS FOR GENERAL USE
1075. PAPER BOARD CARTON
1076. PAPER CONES FOR LOUD SPEAKERS
1077. PAPER FROM AKRA
1078. PAPER FROM BAGASSE WITH CORRUGATED BOARD & BOXES
1079. PAPER FROM BAMBOO
1080. PAPER FROM RICE HUSK AND WHEAT HUSK
1081. PAPER FROM TREE BARK, EUCALYPRUS WOOD
1082. PAPER PRODUCTS
1083. PAPER PLATES, PAPER GLASS
1084. PAPER CUP FOR ICE CREAM
1085. PAPER TUBES SPIRAL WINDING COMPOSIT CONTAINER
1086. PARTICLE BOARD AND BLACK BOARD WITH SANDING & LAMINATION OF PARTICLE BOARD
1087. PARTICLE BOARD FROM RICE HUSK
1088. POUCH FILLING & MAKING FOR TOMATO SAUCE
1089. POUCH MAKING & GRAVURE PRINTING
1090. PROCESSING OF PAPER FOR FEEDING IN COMPUTER
1091. PULP FROM BAMBOO AND WOOD
1092. SAND PAPER
1093. SANITRY NAPKINS
1094. SILICON COATED PAPER
1095. STENCIL PAPER
1096. STRAW BOARD AND GREY BOARD
1096A STRAW BOARD & MILL BOARD
1097. STRAW BOARD AND PAPER BOARD PLANT
1098. TISSUE PAPER FACIAL
1099. TISSUE MOIST TOILETERY CLEANSING TISSUE AND RELATED PRODUCTS
1100. TISSUE PAPER ROLLS
1101. TOILET PAPER ROLLS
1102. TOILET PAPER & NAPKINS
1103. WET FACE FRESHNER TISSUE
1104. WHITE WRITING & PRINTING PAPER
1105. WRITING & PRINTING PAPER (PAPER MILLS)

RUBBER, PLASTIC & POLYMER

1106. ACRYLIC BEADS
1107. ACRYLIC COPOLYMER EMULSION
1108. ACRYLIC LATEX
1109. ACRYLIC SHEET
1110. ACRYLIC SHEET AND MOULDED PRODUCTS
1111. ACRYLIC TEETH
1112. AUTO TUBES
1113. AUTO TYRES & TUBES
1114. B.O.P.P. FILM
1115. B.O.P.P. PRESSURE SENSITIVE SELF ADHESIVE TAPE

Price Rs. 3150/- for each "Detailed Project Report" Payable in advance through Draft/Cash/M.O. in favour of *"ENGINEERS INDIA RESEARCH INSTITUTE"*. 4449, Nai Sarak, Main Road Delhi - 110 006 *OR Ask by V.P.P.* • Ph : 391 8117, 391 6431, 392 0361, 396 0797 •Fax : 91-11- 391 6431 E-Mail : eirisidi@bol.net.in

1116. BABY NIPPLE (SILICON)
1117. BABY NIPPLE (BIG SIZE)
1118. BALLOON PLASTIC ADVERTISING
1119. BLISTER FILM PVC
1120. BLISTER PACKAGING & POUCH PAKAGING
1121. BLOW MOULDING PLASTIC CONTAINER
1122. COATING ON METALIZED POLYESTER FILM/ METALISED PAPER/ ALIMINIUM FOIL
1123. COATING ON PLASTIC (ELECTROLYSIS) & GLASS
1124. COIR FOAM (RUBBERISED)
1125. COLOUR COATING ON PLASTICS
1126. COLOUR MASTER BATCHES FOR VARIOUS PLASTICS
1127. CYCLE TYRES AND TUBES
1128. DISPOSABLE PLASTIC CUPS GLASSES, ETC.
1129. DISPOSABLE PLASTIC SYRINGES WITH NEEDLES
1130. DOUGH MOULDING COMPOUND (D.M.C)
1131. EPOXY RESIN
1132. EXPANDED POLYESTRENE MOULDING (THERMOCOLE)
1133. F.R.P AUTO,SCOOTER ROOFS & CEILINGS
1134. F.R.P PRODUCTS (HELMET, WASHBASIN SHEETS, ROOFING SHEETS)
1135. FIBRE REINFORCED PLASTIC (HIGH PRESSURE MOULDING WITH SMC BMC AND DMC)
1136. FIELD RUBBER CONVERTED TO THE 60% LATEX RUBBER
1137. FLEXIBLE P.U. FOAM
1138. FORMALDEHYDE CROCK -ERY AND OTHER ITEMS
1139. FORMALDEHYDE RESIN (UREA, PHENOL,MELEMINE)
1140. GASKET SHEET
1141. GUM BOTTLE (PVC)
1141A GLASS BEADS
1142. HDPE COATED PAPER SACK
1143. H.D.P.E. CONTAINERS
1144. H.D.P.E. CONTAINERS AND CARBON (BLOW MOULDING)
1145. H.D.P.E. JERRY CANS
1146. HDPE MANUFACTURING FROM ETHYLALCOHOL
1147. H.D.P.E PIPE AND FITTINGS
1148. H.D.P.E. PIPES
1149. H.D.P.E PRINTED BAGS
1150. H.D.P.E TWINES AND ROPES
1151. H.D.P.E. & L.D.P.E PIPES AND FITTINGS
1152. H.D.P.E/PP BOX STRAPPING
1153. H.D.P.E/PP WOVEN SACKS USING PLAIN LOOMS
1154. H.M BAG PLANT WITH PRINTING UNIT
1155. HAWAI CHAPPALS (RUBBER)
1156. I.V PLASTIC BOTTLE
1157. ICE CREAM CUP (PLASTIC)
1157A INJECTION MOULDED AUTO COMPONENTS
1158. INJECTION & BLOW MOULDED PLASTIC PROD.
1159. INJECTION MOULDED PLASTIC PRODUCTS
1159A INTEGERATED COMPLEX ESTER'S & ALLIED PRODUCTS (D.O.P, D.B.P, & ETHYL ACETATE, BUYTL ACETATE, WIRE ENAMELS, JELLY CABLE COMPOUND)
1160. INTEGERATED SURGICAL RUBBER GOODS INDUSTRY
1161. L.D.P.E FROM ETHYL ALCOHOL
1162. LDPE MOULDED PRODUCTS
1163. LAMINATION OF CO-EXTRUSION MULTILAYER FILM IN ROLL FORM
1164. LATEX RUBBER
1165. LATEX RUBBER CONDOM
1166. MASTER BATCHES (COLOURED, P.V.C, L.D.P.E, H.D.P.E, ETC.)
1167. MELAMINE FORMALHYDE RESIN
1168. MOULDED LUGGAGE
1169. MULTI-LAYER (3 LAYER BAGS)
1170. MULTI-LAYER (3 LAYER) FILM WITH LAMINATION & PRINTING
1171. OIL SEAL
1171A PET BOTTLE/CONTAINERS
1172. PTFE COMPONENTS
1173. PU/PVC SOLE FOR SPORT SHOE BY IMPORTED M/C.
1174. PVC BATTERY SEPARATOR
1175. P.V.C COMPOUNDS (FRESH)
1175A P.V.C COMPOUNDS (SCRAP)
1176. P.V.C ELECTRICAL INSULATING TAPE
1177. P.V.C FITTINGS
1178. P.V.C FLEXIBLE FUSIBLE POWDER HEAT FUSIBLE POWDER
1179. P.V.C GRANULES (FOR INSULATION & SHEETS GRADES)
1180. P.V.C GRANULES FROM PVC SCRAPS (WITH POLLUTION CONTROL)
1181. P.V.C HOSES
1182. P.V.C LEATHER CLOTH
1183. P.V.C FLEXIBLE PIPES
1184. P.V.C PIPES AND FITTINGS
1185. POLYTHENE BAGS (PRINTED)
1186. PVC PLASTICS FILM SHEET SOFT/RIGID
1187. PVC RESIN AND COMPOUND
1187A PVC RIGID PIPE
1188. PVC RULAR
1189. PVC STABLIZERS (SINGLE PACK SYSTEM)
1190. PVC WIRE AND CABLES
1191. PAPER BASED PHENOLIC SHEET FOR ELECTRICAL
1192. PHENOL FORMALDEHYDE RESIN
1193. PHENOLIC RESIN
1194. PLASTIC BEADS FROM PLASTIC SCRAPS
1195. PLASTIC BUTTONS
1196. PLASTIC CANS
1197. PLASTIC COLLAPSIBLE TUBE
1198. PLASTIC CORRUGATED SHEET & BOXES
1199. PLASTIC FILM AND SHEETS WITH PRINTING FLEXO & ROTO/LDPE/HDPE/PP/HM/ PVC
1200. PLASTIC GRANULES OR POWDER FROM PLASTIC SCRAP
1201. PLASTIC INJECTION MOULDED T.V. CABINETS
1202. PLASTIC ITEMS-MANUFAC TURE FROM POWDER MELAMINE
1203. PLASTIC GOODS
1203A PLASTIC SHEET FROM SCRAP
1204. PLASTIC PLANT (BLOW MOULDING & INJECTION MOULDING)
1205. PLASTIC PRODUCTS (GOLD, SILVER, NICKEL)
1206. PLASTIC TOYS
1207. POLYESTER BEADING
1208. POLYESTER FILM
1209. POLYTHENE BAGS & AUTOMATIC PRINTING
1210. POLYTHENE PRINTED BAGS
1211. POLYURETHANE FOAM AND ITS PRODUCTS
1212. PROPYLENE FILM (PRINTED) & BAG MANUFACTURING
1212A PLASTIC MATS
1213. RAINBOW COLOUR ON PVC FILM & SHEET
1214. RED MUD PVC PIPES AND FITTINGS
1215. RE-RUBBERISED OF SOLID TYPE
1216. RESIN COATED SAND REXINE
1217. REXINE CLOTH & ALLIED PRODUCTS
1218. RUBBER AUTO PARTS
1219. RUBBER BELTING
1220. RUBBER MOULDING UNIT INCLUDING LINING RUBBER SHEETING
1221. RUBBER RECLAIMING
1222. RUBBER ROLLERS FOR TEXTILE MILLS & PAPER INDUSTRIES
1223. RUBBER SHEET AND ALLIED HOSPITAL RUBBER GOODS
1224. RUBBERIZED PVC GASKET
1225. RUBBERISED COIR
1226. SAFETY BELTS
1227. SILVER AND GOLD PLATING ON PVC AND NYLON-6
1228. SPECTACLE FRAMES (PLASTIC)
1229. SPUNGE RUBBER
1230. SURGICAL EXAMINATION GLOVES
1231. SYNTHETIC PEARL COATING ON POLYSTY RENE BEADS
1232. TEFLON MANUFACTURING
1233. TEFLON TAPE
1234. TEFLON TAPES & CABLES
1235. THERMOCOLE SHEET AND MOULDED PRODUCTS EXPANDED POLYESTERENE EXTRUSION PROFILES
1236. THERFORMED PACKAGING (BLISTER PACKAGING AND POUCH PACKAGING)
1237. THERMOPLASTIC POLYURETHANE
1238. TOOTH BRUSHES
1239. TOY BALLOON, DECORA TIVE AND INDUSTRIAL BALLOONS
1240. TREAD RUBBER
1240A TYRE RETREADING (HOT)
1241. TYRE RETREADING BY COLD PROCESS
1242. TYRE TUBES & FLAPS
1243. UNSATURATED POLYESTER FOR REXINE
1244. V-BELT AND FAN BELT
1245. VINYL ASBESTOS AND PVC WALL PAPER
1246. VITON (FLUORO ELASTOMER)

SOAP, COSMETICS & PERFUMS

1247. ACID SLURRY, SYNTHETIC DETERGENT POWDER
1247A ACID SLURRY
1248. AGARBATTI SYNTHETIC, PERFUMERY COMPOUND
1249. AFTER SHAVE LOTION
1250. ANTISEPTIC CREAM
1251. BETA IONONE
1252. BLEACHING POWDER
1253. BLUE DETERGENT POWDER
1254. CLEANING POWDER (VIMTYPE)
1255. COLD CREAM
1256. COLOURED FLAME & PERFUMED CANDLES (RED, BLUE, GREEN FLAME)
1257. COSMETIC INDUSTRY (MODERN)
1258. COSMETIC INDUSTRY-SHAMPO,SPRAY PERFUME, TALCUM POWDER
1259. DETERGENT POWDER (ARIEL TYPE)
1260. DETERGENT POWDER (NIRMA TYPE) FULLY AUTOMATIC PLANT
1261. DETERGENT WASHING POWDER
1262. FISH OIL SOAP
1263. GLYCERINE TRANSPARENT SOAP
1264. HAIR REMOVING CREAM
1265. HERBAL COSMETICS
1266. HERBAL SHAMPO & CREAM
1267. HERBAL/AYURVEDIC COSMETICS UNIT
1268. INCENSE POWDER,INCENSE STICKS & INCENSE CAKE
1269. OPTICAL WHITENERS
1270. ROSE OIL EXTRACTION
1271. SHAMPOOS (COCONUT OIL BASED COLD PROCESS)
1272. SHAVING CREAM
1273. SINDUR (KUMKUM)
1274. SOAP COATED PAPER
1275. SPRAY DRIED DETERGENT POWDER
1276. STAIN REMOVER
1277. TALCUM POWDER (FACE & TOILET POWDER)
1278. TOILET AND HERBAL SOAP
1279. TOOTH PASTE & POWDER